MAKING PEACE

WITH

CHANGE

NAVIGATING LIFE'S MESSY *Transitions* WITH HONESTY AND GRACE

GINA BRENNA BUTZ

Our Daily Bread
Publishing™

Requests for permission to quote from this book should be directed to: Permissions Department, Our Daily Bread Publishing, PO Box 3566, Grand Rapids, MI 49501, or contact us by email at permissionsdept@odb.org.

Scripture quotations, unless otherwise indicated, are taken from the Holy Bible, New International Version®, NIV®. Copyright © 1973, 1978, 1984, 2011 by Biblica, Inc.™ Used by permission of Zondervan. All rights reserved worldwide. zondervan.com.

Scripture quotations marked ESV are from The Holy Bible, English Standard Version® (ESV®), copyright © 2001 by Crossway, a publishing ministry of Good News Publishers. Used by permission. All rights reserved.

Scripture quotations marked MSG are from *The Message*. Copyright © by Eugene H. Peterson 1993, 1994, 1995, 1996, 2000, 2001, 2002. Used by permission of Tyndale House Publishers, Inc.

Interior design by Sam Carbaugh

Library of Congress Cataloging-in-Publication Data

Names: Butz, Gina Brenna, author.
Title: Making peace with change : navigating life's messy transitions with honesty and grace / Gina Brenna Butz.
Description: Grand Rapids : Our Daily Bread Publishing, 2020. | Summary: "Change is hard. Learn how to rely on God during times of transition and stress. Gina Butz writes with honesty and compassion as she shares personal stories of her struggle with change. Together you'll examine biblical principles that will help you find peace and experience growth through the messiness of change"-- Provided by publisher.
Identifiers: LCCN 2019037895 | ISBN 9781627079716 (paperback)
Subjects: LCSH: Change (Psychology)--Religious aspects--Christianity.
Classification: LCC BV4599.5.C44 B88 2020 | DDC 248.8/6--dc23
LC record available at https://lccn.loc.gov/2019037895

Printed in the United States of America
20 21 22 23 24 25 26 27 / 8 7 6 5 4 3 2

For my husband, Erik,
and our kids, Ethan and Megan.
You're my favorites.

Contents

Introduction

RECENTLY, I TRIED TO TRANSPLANT TWO BUSHES from one part of my yard to another. It seemed simple enough, until I started digging. The roots went much farther and deeper than I had anticipated. They had wrapped themselves around everything surrounding them. I pulled and hacked and wrested those plants out of their homes and crammed them into their new spots. There. Job done.

Needless to say, they did not survive.

Transitions in life are messy like that. When we have to uproot and enter a new season of life, emotional dirt flies. We want to get it over with, to get back to feeling normal. There. Job done. But we feel bruised and broken. We wonder why we're not bouncing back.

A friend of mine told me that when you move a plant, even from one room to another, it's bound to wilt. It needs time to acclimate to its new surroundings. And so do we.

I don't like change. If it had been up to me, I'd still live down the street from my parents, in the town where I grew up. Instead, I've lived in eight different homes in three separate countries. I've been single, married, a parent, a teacher, and a coach, among other roles. My family has lived in our current home for nearly seven years—it's the longest we've lived anywhere. I have become quite familiar with change.

It's tempting to rush through life's transitions—a move to a new city, the death of a loved one, a birth or adoption, a dramatic change in income, health, or job. We want to feel rooted, to know the way, to be established, productive, and confident. We want to feel peace again. And we think that's only found once we're on the other side of these turbulent times. If we can survive that long.

But what if transition is a gift? What if all that uprooting isn't meant to destroy us but to change us?

This book is a call to slow down in the midst of transition. It's an invitation to make peace with change, right in the middle of all its messiness.

Sometimes it takes the turbulence of a transition to shake our hearts loose from the things to which we cling for life. When change happens, parts of our hearts that we can normally ignore, parts deep under the surface, get pulled into the light where we have to face them.

So let's face them together. Let's believe that transition isn't something to endure; it's one of the greatest gifts for our spiritual growth that God can give us. He is the expert gardener. He knows how to guide our hearts through new seasons. These changes—whether chosen or imposed upon us—are necessary and opportune times to weed our hearts and till the soil for new ground. We can emerge more wholehearted—people who believe that God sees and values all of us—so we can bring every aspect of our lives honestly to Him, trusting that He will use it for good.

Jesus promised us abundant life, and that means He wants to take us far beyond just surviving. He calls us to make peace with the change He's bringing us through. Let's be reflective, curious, and full of faith that the transition process can be a redemptive one. God has purpose for us in all of it.

As you read this book, I hope you feel invited to slow down in the midst of the mess of transition. I hope you feel permission to linger honestly in the stirred-up parts of your heart. I hope you meet God there with His extravagant grace. We can do more than just grit our teeth and get through transition. We can experience true peace in it.

CHAPTER ONE

Navigating the Hard

OUR FIRST YEAR OF MARRIAGE WAS KIND OF A piece of cake. (Please don't hate me for that.) Erik and I didn't argue much. On the surface, we did well. But people who met me that year would later describe me as aloof, reserved, and quiet. If you know me well, you know that's not my typical mode. I'm actually quite talkative! I met one of my good friends, Ginger, that year. She thought I didn't even like her. I did, actually. I liked her a lot.

So what was happening? Why was the "real me" hidden from view?

In marrying, I did not just gain a new relationship. I also gained a new city, a new house, new ministry, new team, new church, new everything. None of this was new for my husband. I joined his world. By all accounts, he carried along just fine and I was the one who was shell-shocked. I've heard that when you meet someone in a starkly different new season of life, you should assume that who they are for the first year isn't really them; they're still finding their bearings. Looking back, that rings true for me.

Change is hard on our hearts. It requires heart energy to adjust to new and different ways of living. Meeting new people, finding your way around, adjusting to cultures, carving out new routines—these all take an emotional toll.

Rather than entering into what is hard, we usually stay unaware, as I did. We subconsciously determine to be untouched by our circumstances. We feel solid when things are going well, which doesn't serve us in transition. We have a sense that suffering and pain are wrong, so we don't want to enter into them.

Unfortunately, this is not the way of growth. As a professional counselor and friend, Bruce Edstrom, puts it, "The heart struggling with remaining intact is the heart that, at its core, knows little deep peace, little deep joy, as well as little deep oneness with the Father and others. It fears many things and therefore clings to old familiar structures and ways in a final attempt to keep a sense of identity and control. But it yearns to trust, give freely, and to know the thrill of intimacy. The antidote is, of course, to come to the Father to find what the heart has always been searching for, and trying to provide on its own." [1]

> We have a sense that suffering and pain are wrong, so we don't want to enter into them.

Ignoring the toll transition took on me was easier than feeling the weight of all that I was going through.

Looking back, I realize now that to be at peace with that transition and be wholehearted in the process required me to acknowledge what was happening and how it was impacting me. That much transition in a short period of time is traumatic. It took a toll on my heart. What I was going through was hard. Really, really hard.

CALLING IT HARD

"This is hard." Three simple words we are not inclined to say. To call it hard sounds like we're complaining, and we're not supposed to complain. We're afraid we might turn down a dark road that leads to bitterness and depression. It feels like we're making mountains out of molehills. Making a big deal about ordinary things that people have to go through all the time. We're adults. We should just deal with it. Put on our big-girl panties and get on with life.

Maybe. Or maybe calling it hard allows us to gather parts of our hearts we otherwise would leave behind, and to bring them before God.

This is the first path we must navigate in change. We must call it hard when it is. It is not something we are inclined to do naturally.

We come by this honestly. We are oblivious to how hard something is. We are unaware of how much of our heart energy is being used during times of change in our lives.

When we are unaware, we can't bring our whole hearts to rest in God. Looking back at that first year of marriage, I can see now that I closed down my heart without even knowing it. All that I experienced overwhelmed me. How could it not? I did not have words to acknowledge it, nor did anyone point out to me the weight of what I had just gone through.

So I did what was easiest: I triaged. I pulled back from relationships and life and gave what limited relational energy I could squeeze out of my tight little heart to my husband. No one else had much of a chance.

In time, it got easier. Generally, it does. We learn the new things. We adjust. Ginger learned I truly did like her and wanted to be her friend. The house became our house, the team our team, the church our church. Unfortunately, my lack of awareness of how hard it was kept me from being open to life and others, and actually hurt people in the process. Most of all, it kept me from turning to God for what I needed.

I have seen many people do this—move blindly into significant change—and then wonder why they aren't doing well. It's critical that we learn to acknowledge the impact changes have made on us, and to call them hard when they are hard. This helps us become aware of how our hearts are responding to those changes, and allows us to invite God into the process.

Erik and I experienced lots of change together after that . . . and continue to do so. Not far into our marriage, we moved overseas to work in a country that is closed to the gospel. We spent the next five years planting ourselves there. We became parents, changed jobs, moved homes. It was hard, but we figured out how to live well through all that. Then, when I was finally comfortable, happy, and adjusted, we were uprooted to Singapore. And the hard work of laying down roots started all over again.

Back in the closed country after a five-year absence, we snagged an apartment right next door to our dear friends, Dan and Jenny Higgins and their kids. It was glorious, practically communal living for a year, until they moved back to the States. Another family with whom we'd grown close that year also left the country. We decided to move to another part of town to be closer to remaining friends, but that meant three months of renovating a new apartment. By the beginning of the school year, we had just settled into our new place and started learning new routines of shopping, church, friends, work, and school.

Every other week we hosted a small group in our home with some new people who worked in our office. One week, I asked them to draw pictures of how their hearts were doing at the time, in light of transition. While we were doing this, our ten-year-old son, Ethan, slipped into the room and observed. At one point he came over and said, "Mom, there's something I want to show you."

He had drawn his own picture. It was his bed from above, complete with his fan, clock, books, pillow, and bookshelf. His heart was tucked under the blanket. Zzz's drifted from the smile on its face.

He said, "I drew this because, well, first of all I'm tired and I want to go to bed"—he was a stickler for his bedtime—"but also, because my heart is tired of all the new things."

It took me a second to catalog all that was new that week. When I did, it made complete sense that he was tired. That week alone he had started tae kwon do, language class, the group we were hosting, and a new homeschool co-op where he was the only kid his age, not to mention navigating where he fit in with the neighborhood kids and still grieving the loss of his friends.

Once I began to look at my own heart, I realized I could say the same. All that change wore on me. I sat with God and said, "I feel like too much has been asked of my heart lately." It wasn't a judgment on Him or me. It was simply an acknowledgment of the weight of transition, asking Him to walk it with me. Once again, I let myself call it hard.

We have only to look at the Psalms to see Old Testament examples of people who were honest before God about what they were experiencing. One third of the Psalms are laments—people crying out honestly to God, even raging against Him, in their suffering.

In Psalm 88, which has been called "the blackest of all the laments in the Psalter,"[2] Heman the Ezrahite writes:

> I am overwhelmed with troubles
>   and my life draws near to death.
> I am counted among those who go down to the pit;
>   I am like one without strength.
> I am set apart with the dead,
>   like the slain who lie in the grave,
> whom you remember no more,
>   who are cut off from your care.
>
> You have put me in the lowest pit,
>   in the darkest depths.
> Your wrath lies heavily on me;
>   you have overwhelmed me with all your waves. (vv. 3–7)

This kind of lament seems strange to us, even wrong. Yet it is representative of much of Scripture. Isn't this the kind of complaining that leads us away from faith? Yet there is a difference in this kind of honesty; it keeps God in the picture.

> As Walter Brueggemann says, "Psalm 88 is an embarrassment to conventional faith." The misery being described by Heman in this psalm may well be that of leprosy. Whatever the affliction, as E. Calvin Beisner notes, he "never considers that his sufferings might be the result of chance. He is convinced that they come from God." And he is more than willing to have it out with God over the matter. . . .

Heman's psalm has nothing to do with modern notions of positive confession and self-esteem. Says Beisner, "For people tired of faking it when times get tough, Heman's psalm, dark and dismal as it is, should be a breath of fresh air! It positively reeks with honest misery! He makes no excuses for God. He hides none of his complaints. When he feels abandoned, he says so." [3]

In the New Testament, Paul is our example of someone who admitted how tough life was for him. Of his missionary journey through Asia, he wrote to the church at Corinth, "We were under great pressure, far beyond our ability to endure, so that we despaired of life itself" (2 Corinthians 1:8). And in explaining his commitment to the cause of Jesus Christ, he wrote, "We are hard pressed on every side, but not crushed; perplexed, but not in despair; persecuted, but not abandoned; struck down, but not destroyed" (4:8–9).

Am I trying to say that transition is as challenging as Paul's experiences? Hopefully it isn't! Most of us are not in new seasons because we have been driven there by our enemies or those who persecute us. However, Paul did not ignore the difficulties or put on a brave face. Nor did he allow his experience of hardship to turn him away from God. In fact, his praise was richer because he navigated the hard and still moved toward God. Paul ends by saying, "we do not lose heart" (4:16). This is our desire—that we could call life hard where it is hard and yet not lose heart. How do we do that?

BRINGING WHAT'S HARD TO GOD

One fall, I was training for a half-marathon. A few weeks before the race, my feet started to hurt. I had to spend time after every run stretching and soaking them. I became concerned that I might not be able to run the race. Finally, I called a friend who is a nurse and lifelong runner. When I explained the situation to her, she said, "Gina, you're running long distances. When you run long distances, your feet hurt."

It was so obvious when she said it. I was doing something hard, and it made sense that it would affect me. Armed with this perspective, we can accept (maybe even embrace) the pain as a natural part of the process.

Change brings us to a crossroads. To one side, there is a choice to go through with our hearts intact, untouched, managed. To do that, we have to pretend that life isn't as hard as it seems. We stay blind to the challenges, what they stir in us, and how they impact us. It may be less painful, and we may more quickly get back to being "productive," but we will not experience true peace in the process.

On the other side, we have an opportunity to take a path toward wholeheartedness. Calling it hard is the first step down this path. We learn to say, "Even though this is difficult, this is where God has me, and He can and will use this in my life."

Navigating the hard with honesty means that we need to admit where we are struggling. We name the places where we feel inadequate to the task, weak, confused, uncertain of what He is doing. We name where we are sad, frustrated, fearful, lonely. We name it because it is true, and we would rather bring it to Jesus for help than pretend it's not there.

Calling it hard is not judging it. It's not complaining, doubting God, or looking for a way out. It's simply identifying what it is. Calling it hard gives us permission to face all that is being raised in us—loss, desires, expectations, grief—and to deal with it. We acknowledge where change has turned our lives upside down. It's okay that it's shaken us, that we're not at our "best."

It might be most challenging to admit that transition is hard when we choose to make a change in life and it ends up being more difficult than we imagined. That kind of change can blindside us. We can struggle with shame if we are not thrilled with our new situation, because other people are expecting us to be happy. I have had more than one friend who finally finished a multiyear adoption process, only to find that the instant connection with her child was not there, or her child came with deep issues she was unprepared to face. These friends wrestled with expressing this to anyone for fear that they would hear, "But this is what you wanted!" The same can be true of a promotion, a new relationship, or a new home. Good change—changes we happily choose—can still be hard.

It was in our third year overseas that I hit bottom. Pregnant with my second child, I had intentionally pulled back from responsibilities outside of the home. I didn't realize how that choice would result in loneliness and a feeling of worthlessness. I told a visiting friend, "I could leave and no one could know."

That moment was the first time I hinted to anyone that my new season was hard in a way I didn't know it was going to be. It felt like betrayal to admit I wasn't thrilled with the life I had. I *chose* this.

If we want to love God with all our heart, soul, mind, and strength, we have to bring all of our heart to Him, including the parts that feel hard and resistant to what's happening, the parts where we doubt and are discouraged, where we wrestle and struggle. We bring all of it to Him and believe that He can redeem it. In calling it hard, there's this wild

In calling it hard, there's this wild trust that God can work.

trust that God can work. To encounter hard is not failure. This is exactly what God uses to make us more like Christ.

Theologian D. A. Carson writes, "There is no attempt in Scripture to whitewash the anguish of God's people when they undergo suffering. They argue with God, they complain to God, they weep before God. Theirs is not a faith that leads to dry-eyed stoicism, but a faith so robust it wrestles with God." He points out that the psalmist David, for instance, "does not display stoic resignation, nor does he betray doubt that God exists"; rather, "David's suffering leads him to frank pleading with God, to confession, to tears," and then, "when David breaks through to a new level of confidence" he "wins a renewed knowledge of God, and an assurance that God has heard him and will in fact help." [4] This is what it means to bring our whole heart to God.

Transition is a beautiful opportunity to allow God to minister to *all* of who we are. Throughout this book, we will examine what is stirred in us through change, and how to navigate each of those hard parts with honesty and grace. As we look to God's perspective, strength, wisdom, and provision, we will find peace in this messy process God is bringing us through.

Bringing our hard to Him is the first step in responding well to our hearts in transition.

CHAPTER TWO

Anchored in His Goodness

MY FRESHMAN YEAR OF COLLEGE, I HAD AN AMERICAN history class on Tuesdays and Thursdays. The first day of class, I came back to my room ready to tackle the books. I pulled out the syllabus for that class and saw that for Thursday, just two days later, I was expected to read two whole chapters. I thought surely this was a typo. Our professor could not expect us to read so much in such a short time. Didn't she know we had other classes with work too?

So I called her. Yep. I called her. She told me that indeed, I was to read two chapters. So I did what any self-respecting freshman would do: I called my mom and told her I was quitting school. It was just too hard. I would live with them and work at McDonald's. She quietly listened to my rant and then firmly told me, "You're staying." I knew then that my mother did not love me, and I was on my own.

Sometimes, we don't like the assignments we're given.

ACCEPTING THE ASSIGNMENT

In the summer of 1999, Erik and I traveled to Fort Collins, Colorado, to attend a six-week cross-cultural ministry training. The first weekend we were there, I discovered that I was pregnant. As we stared, pale faced, at the positive sign, Erik optimistically asked, "How accurate are these things?" Um . . . 99 percent? We were pregnant.

I had not planned on being pregnant the summer before we moved overseas. Making the transition to being a mom was not part of my first-year plan. I was supposed to learn a new culture and language and team and ministry. We were going to be team leaders for the first time. That seemed like enough transition to navigate already. How was I supposed to do all that with a baby? As my mother-in-law put it, "Wow, Gina. Your first year as a missionary and your first year as a mom. Wow."

Yeah, wow. I had no idea what I was about to go through.

All I knew was that this was not the plan. I honestly contemplated, briefly, that this might be the one time in history God made a mistake. Like, He looked away for a second and, oops, I got pregnant. (I know, I know.) I just couldn't see how becoming a mom would be a good transition in my life at that time.

As I lay awake night after night that summer, crying into my pillow and wondering how on earth this was going to work, God brought the words of a song to mind, a song based on Psalm 16:

> Keep me safe, O God,
>   for in you I take refuge.

I said to the LORD, "You are my Lord;
    apart from you I have no good thing." . . .

LORD, you have assigned me my portion and my cup;
    you have made my lot secure.
The boundary lines have fallen for me in pleasant places;
    surely I have a delightful inheritance. . . .

Therefore my heart is glad and my tongue rejoices;
    my body also will rest secure. (vv. 1–2, 5–6, 9 NIV 1984)

That song ran over and over in my mind. God promised me something through it. He told me that this was His assignment for me. And that it was good. It was just the right amount for me at that season of life. It was from the hands of a good and sovereign God who loves me and knows me and gives me what is best for me. His timing is perfect. His plans come at just the right time—not necessarily my timing, but the timing chosen by One infinitely wiser than me.

God was asking me to rest secure in it.

I essentially responded, "Prove it."

And God responded: Challenge accepted.

I could write for hours about how God has proven the goodness of that assignment. We experienced His timing as I went into labor just hours before our new friends Dan and Jenny arrived in our new country, needing a place to stay. Their son, Jackson, only three months old, became Ethan's best friend (and they are close to this day). Dan and Jenny, also new team leaders on a nearby college campus, became our companions as we walked through the lessons of culture, language, ministry, and parenting. We did life together.

Was it a hard transition to being a mom? One of the toughest I have made. But in the back of my mind was the assurance, "This is for my good." It was true then, and it continues to be true.

We can navigate the hard and make peace with change when we are confident that every part of transition—every moment, interaction, emotion, challenge, surprise—is from the hands of a loving Father. He calls us to rest in His goodness and sovereignty. Everything is meant to help us grow.

Often what stumps us in transition, what keeps us from diving in and embracing it wholeheartedly, is that we don't receive it as an assignment from Him. And not an ordinary assignment but a "given from the hands of the One who loves you more than life, who works all things for your good" kind of assignment.

Granted, it's not always easy to see it that way. I vividly remember standing on a street corner in Asia with three-month-old Ethan strapped to my chest, trying to wave down taxi after taxi in my effort to get to the hospital for a checkup. At least five taxis I hailed were taken by some stranger standing beside me with no compassion for the new mama. Through gritted teeth, I repeated over and over, "This is assigned. This is assigned. This is assigned."

> Every part of transition—every moment, interaction, emotion, challenge, surprise—is from the hands of a loving Father.

But embracing our assignment doesn't mean white-knuckled, gritted-teeth acceptance. We find solid ground when we fall on His goodness.

GOD AT WORK IN OUR ASSIGNMENT

After ten years of friendship, we were a week away from saying goodbye to the Higgins family. After our sons, we had both had girls who also became fast friends. We had only been back from Singapore in the same location with them for one year, and as we faced this goodbye, Ethan asked me, "Mom, why did God bring us back here if He was just going to take them away?"

In looking at the hard aspects of this transition, it was natural for him to question God's hand. I was speechless in the moment.

As I walked around our neighborhood later that morning, I was reminded of the promises God gave me through Psalm 16. I shared those verses with our son. We talked about what it means to have an assignment, to have a portion that is measured out just for us. We talked about the boundaries around a property and how they keep us safe and show us where we are supposed to be. And we talked about how all these things are from the hands of a good God who loves us and wants the best for us.

We talked about how this assignment from God might work out for our good. Our friends leaving meant that we were also moving to another part of town, closer to our office. My husband's commute would be literally a four-minute walk from door to desk instead of an hour by subway. We would have more time as a family, be closer to friends, and have more connection with our team. And that was only what we could see—who knew what else God had in store? We reflected about how it had been a good chapter of our lives, given to us by God. We talked about previous chapters that weren't as great, but we could see how God brought us through. And we ended by confirming our belief that whatever is in the next stage, God is there. We sat with "this is hard" and "God is at work for our good." When we put both together, we could rest.

We can probably all mentally assent to the truth of God's goodness; what trips up many of us is that we have strongly held ideas of what goodness looks like. Embracing His goodness means embracing the means by which He accomplishes good in our lives. It also means aligning ourselves with His agenda for us.

The move to our second overseas assignment was a challenging one; we loved our first assignment and hadn't been looking for a change. But God provided a wonderful community, both through work and at church, that sustained us through our transition.

Three years in, though, many of those friends moved away, and due to rising rent costs, we were forced to move to a new apartment. It was the first time overseas that we hadn't lived in community with other expatriate coworkers. The kids were used to having other American children next door, down the hall, a floor below.

Ethan went through mild depression that year, at the tender age of seven. Midway through our first year in that apartment, I developed allergies. I tried every over-the-counter medication available for a few months, and finally went to an allergist, who told me I had developed a severe allergy to dust mites. He put me on an experimental drug touted to cure all allergies within a year (it had no effect on me) and a daily prescription drug that I had to take immediately upon waking. If I didn't, my allergies took over and I was useless.

We have strongly held ideas of what goodness looks like.

As a homeschool mom with a husband who traveled extensively, I was falling apart. This felt like a bum assignment, one that I was ready to move on from. As I sat on my living room couch one morning, trying to navigate this new hard, I said to God, "Please make it easier. I know you could make it easier."

I felt the Holy Spirit impress on me, "What you're really saying is, 'I don't want to have to need you *this much*.'"

My agenda was clearly different from God's. I wanted my comfort, my happiness. I knew God could use it to shape me, but at that moment I didn't care about my character; I didn't want hard anymore. I wanted His goodness to look the way I envisioned.

We don't receive transitions as assignments when our own agenda trumps God's. When we focus on the world's values of happiness and success and comfort, we aren't in line with God's syllabus for us. We make it our goal to eliminate all the challenges and move on.

In my school of life, the assignments would all be easy, and I could ace the class. God's desired outcome for our lives is not our comfort but our character, not our happiness but our transformation. His assignments line up perfectly with moving us toward those outcomes.

God moved us into that new season, and it became the impetus for us to move back to where we'd previously lived, a dream that had been stirring in us for two years. In fact, it forced some changes in our overall ministry that were necessary, and we helped start a new office location. Looking back, I can see how God used that season not only to help me grow but also to bring about greater good.

We don't always have the big picture. Becoming a mom when I did—that didn't just change my life in that moment, it has had ripple effects in all the time since. Each assignment from God is only one small part of a greater picture, a woven tapestry of God's work in the world.

RESTING IN GOD'S GOODNESS

Doubting God's agenda points to a deeper issue: doubting that God does indeed want good for us. Romans 8:31 asks, "If God is for us, who can be against us?" Often, the real question we have is not "Who can be against us?" but "*Is* God for us?"

Many times, when I have been brought to new circumstances in my life—my unexpected pregnancy, friends moving away, international moves I wasn't seeking—I was asking that question: Is God really in this? Can this situation which I would not have chosen actually be evidence of the goodness of God?

We have to embrace this truth: He is good even if we do not see it. This is where we find peace.

The psalmist David embraced this truth when he said, "Surely your goodness and love will follow me all the days of my life, and I will dwell in the house of the LORD forever" (Psalm 23:6). Wherever God takes you, whatever new chapter crops up in your life, however your roles might change, His agenda is marked by His goodness and mercy toward you every step of the way.

In *The Sacred Romance*, Brent Curtis and John Eldredge share their view of a loving God who relentlessly pursues—romances—our hearts: "'God is good,' the Romance tells us. 'You can release the well-being of your heart to Him.'" [1]

We can release the well-being of our hearts to Him. We can open our hands and surrender to His agenda. We can embrace this assignment because He is good. We see Him in the challenges, using them for our growth. He is for us. Resting in Him requires faith in the moments when we can't see the goodness.

When we told our son that we were moving back to the States years later, he literally crumpled onto the floor and cried (he may have inherited a propensity for the dramatic

He is good even if we do not see it.

from his mother). He couldn't see any good in this move. It was taking him away from everything good he knew. We had to call him back to believing in God's goodness, and leaning on His sovereignty in the path He has us on.

Sometime during the summer before we moved back to the States, I read the story of Moses sending the spies ahead into Canaan. All but two of them came back with a report that, although the land was flowing with milk and honey, the people there were strong and the cities fortified and large. These latter aspects were enough to discourage them from entering.

Thankfully, Joshua and Caleb took a stand:

> Joshua son of Nun and Caleb son of Jephunneh, who were among those who had explored the land, tore their clothes and said to the entire Israelite assembly, "The land we passed through and explored is exceedingly good. If the LORD is pleased with us, he will lead us into that land, a land flowing with milk and honey, and will give it to us. Only do not rebel against the LORD. And do not be afraid of the people of the land, because we will devour them. Their protection is gone, but the LORD is with us. Do not be afraid of them." (Numbers 14:6–9)

They had seen how hard it was going to be, but they were anchoring their faith in the goodness of God who had called them to take the land. The Israelites could move into the promised land not because of their strength or because it was going to be easy, but because God delighted in them and was with them. God is good to those who seek Him in transition, to those who put their hope not in strong coping skills or the promise of a better job or the support of friends to get them through (though all those may help) but in Him alone. There is good to come.

I read that story around the time Ethan was struggling the most with his new assignment to America. He's a realist, like me (it sounds so much better than "pessimist"), and he was anticipating the difficulties of transitioning to new friends, new places.

I shared the story with him because when I read it, I felt clearly that God was saying, "Who will you be like, Gina? Will you look ahead and see only the obstacles, or will you look ahead with faith and hope because you believe I am leading you to this place?"

In the end, though the details of each transition look different— new geography, new roles, new vocation—we can move into them with this perspective: God is bringing us to a new place where He will show us His goodness. He delights in us, and He is with us.

This passage tells us that the way to anchor ourselves in God's goodness in transitions is to approach them with faith. We embrace them fully. We acknowledge what is hard because we trust that it comes from a good and sovereign God who knows the boundaries that will bring us life. We don't know what this new season will bring, but God does, and that is enough. He sees the good He plans to do for us. When we embrace the idea that God can bring good things in a new season, we see them with eyes of faith. We find good in the assignment, even in what is hard.

GOD KNEW THIS WOULD HAPPEN

At one point in our time overseas, as we enjoyed the fellowship of a group of people previously unknown to us, it occurred to me, "God knew this would happen."

It caused me to wonder what God would say to us, going into a transition, if He told us all the good things He had in store. He would say things like, "Oh, but Gina, you're going to meet your new best friend" or "You wouldn't believe how much you'll love this church" or "You have no idea how much I am going to grow you in this season."

Just recently, I shared these thoughts with a new friend of mine. She is one of my "Oh, but Gina" people. I had no idea I would meet her, but God knew. She is part of this current assignment, and she is such a blessing.

I can see the goodness of God in this transition back to the United States. I stand in the middle of Ethan's room, looking around at the mementos he has on his walls: awards from teachers at his new school, photos of friends he didn't know before, schedules for new activities he didn't do overseas. We eat dinner with friends we didn't know, we are greeted by friendly faces at church, someone saves us a place at the soccer game—these are all part of this current assignment. God foresaw these blessings. He planned them in advance for us.

We didn't know *what* they would be, but we could have faith they *would* be. We have met God in new ways. We have experienced new aspects of His character. We have seen Him once again faithfully provide what we need financially, spiritually, emotionally, socially. We are a blessed people who go through repeated transitions and are able to see God show up in His glory and goodness again and again.

Faith carries us in the "not yet" places. We have to believe that the challenges we encounter in transition can be used for good in our lives. We know it intellectually, but it can be so painful to embrace. We hold to the blessings, but we are called to move into the hard as well, because it is all part of the assignment. We experience God's character as He pours out His blessings in new seasons, but the potential to experience Him is even greater in the harder aspects of transition. If we move into transition with faith, we are more likely to see and respond with open hearts to all of what God is giving us.

Maybe where you are is not where you had planned to be. Maybe it's a tough road. But rest in this: not only is this His assignment for you, but He is with you in it. He won't ask you to go anywhere without Him. He has gone ahead to prepare something for you, for your transformation, to make you more like Jesus. You can share your struggles with Jesus and rest in His goodness.

When we moved back to the States, I heard about this practice many embrace of choosing a word to focus on for the year. I wasn't sure how to choose one, so a friend of mine suggested that I consider what word kept coming to mind.

"Overwhelmed." But that seemed like a poor choice. Maybe I could aim for "underwhelmed" instead? My friend then encouraged me to think of what I needed in the coming year.

"Chocolate." I felt like that would carry me through a lot. By the same reasoning, my husband decided his word should be "beef."

When I thought about it more, I wanted to choose a word like "settled" or "rooted" or "known." That was what I wanted to feel. In the end, God gave me the word "content." His voice pressed on me: "Gina, what if you aren't settled? What if you don't feel known yet? Will you receive whatever it is I give you this year with a trusting heart?" It was not the word I was hoping for, but it shifted my heart away from focusing on what I did not have and onto what He was giving me. I could be content by anchoring in His goodness. In that way, I could make peace with this change.

Whatever new assignment you've been given is good, because He is good. He is there. He is in it. He has gone before. Let's enter change with faith that whatever challenges it brings, He will use for good in our lives.

CHAPTER THREE

Navigating Loss

LIFE IN CENTRAL FLORIDA IS MADE SIGNIFICANTLY more comfortable in the summer months when your house includes a backyard pool. Sometimes, I lie in a floating chair in our pool and let myself drift around. I know I can't go far because it's not a big pool. Soon enough I'll hit a side and float in another direction.

Transitions pull us out of our known, contained pools and drop us into an ocean. What once gave us definition is gone. Lost. We are adrift. Insecure. When we feel this, our desire naturally is to reestablish those boundaries as quickly as possible. We want something manageable, something with defined edges. The walls of our pools are the roles, relationships, and abilities we have that give shape to who we are. They are what give us a sense of identity. It takes a long time in any season to feel comfortable with who we are. Losing our identity can be disheartening. We desperately want to find those familiar edges again.

In our transition back to the United States, I incurred more losses than at any other time. I felt like I was drifting on a tiny raft, with no land in sight, a little like Tom Hanks in *Cast Away* (though at no point did I make a disemboweled volleyball my confidante—thankfully, it never came to that). I longed for the edges, the boundaries, the things that make me say, oh right, this is where I am, where I belong, who I am, what I'm capable of. I found myself looking to others to say, "Here's land." I sought affirmation, acknowledgment, value, anything to make me feel grounded again. In each transition, I have lost that to some extent, and I imagine you have too.

Our losses reveal our hearts. Before we rush back to rebuilding our manageable backyard pools, it's important to reflect on them. I can understand the temptation not to do so. Looking at what I've lost seems like a terrible idea. It sounds depressing, sad, and likely to make me wallow in self-pity. Wouldn't it just be better to focus on our gains?

I'm all for gains, but I have found there to be purpose and heart growth in first examining the losses we have sustained through transition. Why? Because whether or not we acknowledge them, our losses impact us. And those losses must be grieved. We must give ourselves permission to mourn what we had and no longer have. Grief, however, is a topic that needs its own space, so we'll come back to it in chapter 9. For now, as we look at navigating our losses, there is value in examining what the losses we feel tell us about ourselves. Where you feel loss most acutely says something about how you are living your life, where you are putting your deepest value, and what has defined you.

Our losses reveal our hearts.

In examining loss, we'll see more clearly where we've looked outside of ourselves for definition. We all have well-worn paths we take toward that which makes us feel whole. God should be at the end of that path; it's our human nature to take divergent ones. When we look at what we have lost, we begin to recognize what feels like life to us, but which in fact is a poor substitute for the true life found in Him. As we allow the Lord to build us back up, to redefine our lives, He gives us a more solid foundation.

LOSS OF CONNECTION: "WHO KNOWS ME?"

A few years into our time back in the States, our daughter, Megan, joined a new soccer team. Upon arriving at their first scrimmage, I realized that I didn't even know which set of parents belonged to our team. I parked my chair, pulled out my phone, and called my friend, Kourtney, so I wouldn't look completely alone. After half an hour, I discerned I was with the wrong people. I was feeling the loss of connection.

Perhaps the most significant losses we incur are with regard to others. Whether we thrive most with a large group of people we know, or are more content with a few deeper friendships, few of us choose isolation. We were made to live in relationship with people. We come to rely on others for a sense of being known and loved. Those relationships meet heart-level needs and give us a sense of who we are.

Connection happens in big ways and small ways. It's going to church and having people greet you by name. It's having that everyday friend you know you can text when things are tough. It's neighbors you can call on for help, small groups, fellow parents, friendly coworkers. We are created with a desire to belong. We long to be known, for people to care that we are present. When we have this connection, it can carry us through some of the most difficult challenges.

Sometimes our transitions take us physically away from friends and families. As much as we may desire and attempt to maintain these connections, they change and we feel that loss.[1] But connection is not just something we lose when we move. Any change in our roles also affects how we relate to others. I had to navigate loss of connection when I got married and wasn't sure how to relate to my single friends anymore, and when I became a mom and it suddenly felt like hunting down a unicorn to have a deep conversation with a friend or meaningful time with my husband. These changes brought blessing, of course, but I was unprepared for how they would change my relationships with others. This is something worth acknowledging.

This loss has even been felt when we have moved back to situations where we were previously known, where we already had some relationships from the past. In our absence our friends had formed new relationships, filling the space we had previously taken. Their relational energy was at capacity, and it was uncertain how we would fit back into their lives. That process, too, may involve grieving how things used to be.

There's a deeper knowing for which we were designed as well. It is a knowing that tends to take more time to develop, aside from the rare occasions when it seems natural to grab someone's hand and jump into the deep end of the pool. We are meant to be known at our core. Tim Keller writes, "To be loved but not known is comforting but superficial. To be known and not loved is our greatest fear. But to be fully known and truly loved is, well, a lot like being loved by God. . . . It liberates us from pretense, humbles us out of our self-righteousness, and fortifies us for any difficulty life can throw at us." [2] It is when life throws these difficult changes our way that we most need to feel loved and known, yet it can be the time when we feel we've lost this.

We move into a new season, and people may know and recognize us on a superficial level, but we long for the people and places where we can fully be ourselves, where people have walked through deep waters with us and not left our sides. We crave the connection of people who love us as we are.

It's important to remember that we were made for this, for deep connection. In Genesis 2:18, God looked at creation and said, "It is not good for the man to be alone. I will make a helper suitable for him." And He made woman. From the beginning, God designed us for relationship. When we lose those human connections, we have lost something for which we were designed.

Loss of Competence: "I don't know how."

One day early in our time overseas, I rode my bike to the grocery store. After parking in the "bike corral" and paying the bike guard to "guard" my bike (many experiences overseas require air quotes), I went to shop. When I came back out, I couldn't find my bike. A little miffed at the guard for losing my bike (after all, I did pay him, albeit very little), I asked him in my limited language skills, "Where is my bike?"

He responded with an explanation that I could not understand, so I asked again, "Where is my bike?"

Again, he told me where it was, but I didn't understand what he said. This went back and forth several times. I guess I was hoping he would finally say something different that I *did* understand but that didn't happen.

Finally, he shouted at me, "Oh, you don't understand!"

"You're right! I don't understand! I don't understand!" I cried back. *That* I could understand.

Loss of competence causes us to cry out, "I don't understand this! I don't know how to do this!" It wasn't just my lack of language competence that tripped me that day; it was not understanding the culture of how bike guards work. I was no longer competent at simple, basic activities. What I realized that day was how important it is for us to feel like we know what we're doing.

We take for granted being able to do a job well, to live life like we know what we're doing. Transition has the potential to take away that feeling of confidence, and it's not just when we move to another culture. Any new situation can strip us of the feeling that we have what it takes.

Maybe you're a new parent, and all the baby books in the world don't really tell you what to do at 2 a.m. when he *just won't sleep.* Maybe you thought you knew how to do this new job, but things run differently at the new office and you're feeling a bit lost. This new city doesn't have the same stores you knew back home, or the same doctors, or the same anything, and you feel like you're starting from scratch. The new church doesn't sing the same songs. Your spouse was the one who did the taxes and now you're alone and you don't have a clue where to start.

Whoever we are, transition can leave us feeling incompetent. It can be difficult to admit this, because as we look around, it seems like other people have it down. Maybe we've read the books and thought we were prepared. We didn't realize life would be so different in this new place.

I was surprised by the ways I felt incompetent when we returned to our homeland. After all, I'm an American; I should know how to do life here! But I had spent most of my adult life overseas, adapting to the norms of other cultures. I had never been a parent here. When I was asked to provide proof of immunization to our children's school, I realized I had immunization records from four different countries. Accustomed to being able to call a doctor and get a same-day appointment, I naively called a new pediatrician and asked if my children could be seen that week. The receptionist laughed at me; I could get an appointment in a month. Experiences like this in our transition pointed to my loss of competence even in my own culture. In so many new situations, we just don't know the ropes.

Loss of competence can leave us feeling foolish, frustrated, and fearful of failure. It's okay to feel like we don't know what we're doing. We *don't* know what we're doing! Why should we? It's new. It's different. It takes time. There's a learning curve to every new season.

In the meantime, we remind ourselves of this: "Such confidence we have through Christ before God. Not that we are competent in ourselves to claim anything for ourselves, but our competence comes from God" (2 Corinthians 3:4–5).

Even the apostle Paul did not consider himself competent to minister the gospel; he acknowledged that all of his competence came from God. As believers in Jesus Christ, that's our admission too. And I believe it applies to every area of our lives, not just actively witnessing for Jesus Christ. Whatever confidence we had in functioning well in our previous season of life, it was a gift from God. To face our losses is an opportunity to see what He gave us and to be grateful for what we had. In this place, we can acknowledge our need for Him to be our competence again. Navigating our losses brings us to our humanity.

> Loss of competence can leave us feeling foolish, frustrated, and fearful of failure.

Loss of Contribution: "Where is my place?"

When my husband changed to a new job our third year overseas and I was pregnant with Megan, I pulled back from all ministry responsibilities. Suddenly, no one was depending on me for work apart from my one-year-old. The things I considered my gifts and talents lay dormant.

I had not considered how that change would hit me, how stepping away from ministry would impact my sense of contribution, of having something to offer. (And even if I did, I wouldn't have known what to do differently.) We were created for good works, and we long to have purpose and meaning in our lives. It is another major area where we tend to feel loss.

Many new parents, especially mothers, have to let go of parts of our jobs, ministries, or volunteer opportunities, at least for some time or in some capacity. We can't always do what we did before. Maybe it's because we don't have time. Maybe it's because we no longer have opportunity. Maybe it's inconvenient or even impossible. Maybe it's because no one is asking. Maybe it's just not what we are called to do anymore.

When we returned to the States, I did not immediately find opportunities to contribute. We moved because Erik accepted a job offer; there was no corresponding offer for me. While our ministry intentionally wanted to give me grace and space to transition, I deeply longed for someone to say, "Here is a place for you. Here is where you can use your gifts."

One day, a neighbor emailed me to ask if we would be willing to host her son for a weekend while she and her husband went away for some prayer and planning. She communicated that I need not feel obligated, and that she felt guilty asking me since we were new.

I couldn't say yes fast enough. She had no idea what a blessing it was to feel like I could give to someone else!

Paul tells us in Ephesians 2:10, "For we are God's handiwork, created in Christ Jesus to do good works, which God prepared in advance for us to do." We have been created for a purpose, and when we live that out, we give glory to God. That word, *handiwork*, sometimes translated *workmanship*, is the Greek word *poiēma*, from which we have the word "poem."

Poetry is a work of art, beautifully crafted by its author. This verse tells us we are called to offer who we uniquely are and what we are capable of doing to the world. When others don't see us for who we are, or invite us to share our offerings, it can be painful. It is important for us to see where we feel we have lost this.

Loss of Identity: "Who am I?"

Whether we like it or not, the prior three areas—connection, competence, and contribution—provide definition to who we are as people. Our relationships provide support and a place to belong. Our skills help us navigate the world with confidence. And having our efforts make a difference allows us to see ourselves as an important part of the greater picture. The loss of these three adds up to a loss of identity.

Throughout our lives, we unconsciously ask fundamental identity questions: What must I do to find my place? What gives me significance? What do I have to do to find love and belonging? We learn—from parents, teachers, friends, life experience—what it takes for us to feel that we are loved and significant. The problem is that the answers to these questions are often formed out of a desire for self-protection and self-promotion. Even if we meet God at an early age, it is our human nature to find the answers on our own.

In *The Magnificent Defeat*, Frederick Buechner writes about this process, identifying it as one of two battles that wage in our hearts:

> All our lives we fight for a place in the sun—not a place in the shadows where we fear getting lost in the shadows and becoming a kind of shadow ourselves, obscure and unregarded. . . . We fight to be visible, to move into a place in the sun, a place in the family, the community, in whatever profession we choose, a place where we can belong, where there is light enough to be recognized as a person and to keep the shadows at bay. The Germans use the word lebensraum, room to live in. [3]

We have learned what it takes for us to find our "place in the sun." If we ponder the roles we play in relationships, particularly with our family of origin, we see clues to how we have answered those questions of identity: perhaps "I'm the black sheep of the family" or "I was the golden child." We figure out the roles we have to play to feel secure: the funny one, the strong one, the helpful one, the good kid, the one who didn't rock the boat. These roles, whether we realize it or not, become part of who we feel compelled to be in order to make life work.

In new chapters of our lives, we can no longer operate the way we always have; we've lost the way to those well-worn paths of comfortable living. *How can I be the strong one when I actually feel weak and helpless? How do I live as the helpful one when I don't know anyone to help? How can I be the competent person I've always been when I don't know how life works here?* Often, transition doesn't allow us to be who we have always found comfort in being, and that, my friends, is a merciful gift from God.

The blessing of navigating loss is that it opens our eyes to how we've been defining ourselves.

Relationships are important. It's a gift to be a parent, a friend, a leader. But that is not who you are.

It's a gift to know your world and move through it with confidence. But your abilities should not define you.

It's a gift to have your niche in life, to know you make an impact on your world. But we shouldn't try to measure our impact and draw self-worth from it.

All those things may change. We have to hold them loosely. If God takes them away, that's okay.

In the novel *The Expatriates* by Janice Y.K. Lee, a character who has been transplanted to a new life in Hong Kong observes, "When everything you thought was yours was taken away, and the foundation of your life shifted so you have to start from zero, you might find out who you really are."[4] This is the invitation we find in navigating loss: to let go of who we thought we were to find who we truly are.

> Often, transition doesn't allow us to be who we have always found comfort in being, and that is a merciful gift from God.

RECOGNIZING GOD AND FINDING OURSELVES

There is perhaps no more heartbreaking story of loss in Scripture than that of Job. Job was known for being blameless and upright. He had seven sons and three daughters, and by the sounds of it, they were a close family who enjoyed doing life together. He was wealthy and successful. He was described as "the greatest man among all the people of the East" (Job 1:3). Then, in the span of a short time, he lost it all.

First, his livestock were all stolen or destroyed, taking away his livelihood. Next, his role as a father was taken away in a moment when all his children died. As he is mourning these losses, Satan delivers another blow by attacking his health. In the course of bringing these losses to the Lord, his relationships with his wife and friends become strained. There was no area of his life where he did not feel loss.

We see in Job's response an example of what it looks like to navigate loss. Job does not hold back from mourning, from crying out to God in his distress, yet he holds on to his integrity by re-membering, "The LORD gave and the LORD has taken away; may the name of the LORD be praised. . . . Shall we accept good from God, and not trouble?" (1:21; 2:10).

Job recognized that what he had was from God. He did not shy away from expressing his grief in losing all of it, yet he held on to his faith. He held on to God and wrestled with Him about what all this loss meant for him. He praised and he questioned. He looked the losses full in the face in the light of who God is.

We can follow Job's example in finding ourselves again as we examine our losses and what they are saying to us, allowing ourselves to mourn what we have lost in the process, and then turning our eyes back to the One who gave it all to us in the first place.

In my most recent transition, connection was a challenge for me at first. It looked so different than it did in my previous seasons, and I struggled to feel known. Loneliness—a common problem in transition—became an unwelcome companion. Our kids left one summer on a monthlong mission trip, giving me a taste of what it will be like when they leave for college. Some people look forward to the empty nest stage; I'm terrified of it. I know that losing something of this role as a mom will bring loneliness back into the picture and take away parts of what I have offered to others.

But loneliness is a teacher. It reminds us that this desire for relationship is God-given and good. It calls us to solitude, which can be a challenge. Yet, there we meet God and renew our relationship with Him. It reminds us that no human relationship, however good it is, will ever satisfy the way God does. Solitude calls us back to rest in Him.

The same holds true for losing places of competence. It teaches us to be humble, willing to admit what we do not know, to take risks to ask others to help us. Self-sufficiency can cover a lie that we must keep it together, that if we reach out in need, it's possible no one will answer. But in this vulnerable place of loss, God gives us the opportunity to trust that He will provide, if not through someone else, then through himself. Loss of competence teaches us that it is okay to be helpless, weak, and needy.

It's painful not to have something to offer our world, as happens when we lose opportunities to contribute. But when we are stripped of what we can offer outside of ourselves, we are brought back to the truth that who we are alone is a great gift to the world. Our presence, our emotions, even our messy selves can be a blessing to others.

All of it reminds us we are not what we do. We are not what others think of us. We are not defined by what we can offer or by who knows us. These losses can unveil lies we believe about what we must do or be or have in order to be secure.

The good news is that we can make peace, even with our losses. God is calling us to find ourselves in a deeper place, on the solid ground of who He is and who we are in Him.

CHAPTER FOUR

Anchored in What Is Constant

DURING ONE OF OUR LAST WEEKS IN ASIA, I WAS driving a new friend around town and she said, "I can't wait until I know this city like you do. You seem to know how to get everywhere." Indeed, it was familiar to me. Eight years in one place will do that to you.

In our first few weeks in Orlando, I found myself longing for that kind of knowledge. I wanted to be able to sense—as I drove down the 417 toward our house—how much farther it was to our exit. When I had a need, I wanted to instinctively know which store or service provider could meet it. I wanted to be able to drive on mental autopilot to other parts of town. I wanted familiarity.

In the midst of my longing to know this place, God reminded me of this fact: I already have something familiar and it is Him. As we navigate our losses, we can find comfort and security in focusing on the unchangeable aspects of our lives; doing so has been one of the greatest sources of joy and strength for me in transition. There are only two elements of our lives that do not change: who God is and who we are in relation to Him.

He Is Our Solid Ground

All too often in transition, we can feel as though our path is hidden, as though we've lost our footing. In Isaiah 40:27–28, we read God's response in a time when Israel felt this keenly: "Why do you say, Israel, 'My way is hidden from the LORD; my cause is disregarded by my God'? Do you not know? Have you not heard? The LORD is the everlasting God, the Creator of the ends of the earth. He will not grow tired or weary, and his understanding no one can fathom."

This verse is an awesome truth for us in new seasons of life. We lose our bearings, our sense of identity, our comfortable places. We are staring at the unfamiliar. New seasons even unveil ways we have wandered off on our own, relying on ourselves to find life. This is our reminder that there is solid ground beneath in the presence of the Creator of the earth.

In every new place, He is there. He is the same here as He was in the last season, in the last location. His character and His ways toward us are steady and unchanging. This is where we can hang our hat, even before we put hooks on the walls of our new homes, or know which way to go in a new situation. The struggle is learning to rest in it.

I once heard a speaker at a Bible camp talk about his experience with a friend named Pete. He and Pete had jobs with a logging company, the details of which are fuzzy to me, but it involved getting logs into a stream. On occasion, for fun, they would ride the logs down the stream for a bit. One beautiful lazy day, they lingered on the logs a bit too long and realized they had come into rough waters. So rough, in fact, that they were not confident they could get to shore.

Dave, the speaker, asked his friend what he was going to do. Having been a swimmer in college, Pete decided to try for shore. Dave could see that even with Pete's skill, it was a struggle. He thought, "What am I going to do? I can't swim that well!" Meanwhile, the water moved faster and became increasingly turbulent.

Pete ran along shore, encouraging Dave to try to swim. Seeing the danger ahead, Dave made a break for it and began paddling as hard as he could for shore. He was getting nowhere. Pete continued to run alongside and shout but the words were lost in Dave's frantic splashing.

> There are only two elements of our lives that do not change: who God is and who we are in relation to Him.

Finally, Dave decided to give up. He could see the rapids ahead. He was a goner. Why fight it? So he went limp. At that moment, he could finally hear Pete's words, "Stand up, Dave! Stand up!"

So Dave stood and walked to shore.

Whenever I recall this story, I see myself. I see how frantically I try to work to get life in order, to get to solid ground, when all the while it is right there underneath me if I would only rest in it. God, for some reason, often chooses to speak to us in what Elijah experienced in 1 Kings 19 as the "gentle whisper" (v. 12). We can't hear it when we are scrambling on our own. We must learn to plant our feet firmly on the solid ground in transition—the solid ground of who He is.

After the year of focusing on the word *content*, I chose another word for the new year. The word that kept coming to mind was *abide*. Fueled by this need for solidness, I knew that God was calling me to anchor myself in Him before I moved any further into this new season.

Found in the English Standard Version of John 15:5, *abide* means, "to dwell, to remain, to stay." Jesus calls us to abide in Him, a good word for those of us who have been uprooted and long for a solid place. The more we remain in Him and stay with His truth, the more secure we will feel.

Throughout that year, I wrestled with what it truly means to abide in Him. What does it look like, practically speaking?

Sometimes, it's as simple as remembering that He is with us.

THE GOD WHO IS WITH US

When we first moved overseas, I spent many mornings walking around the campus where we lived for exercise. I brought my headphones and Walkman (for you younger folks, that was a portable tape player, and yes, with cassette tapes). In this place where most people had never heard the name of Jesus, I would pray and listen to worship music. One day, I noticed people staring at me more than usual (local people were fascinated by my white skin, blue eyes, and pregnant belly). I realized I had accidentally pressed the button on my Walkman that broadcast the music publicly. No wonder they were staring at the crazy foreign woman.

Many days as I walked and worshipped, I tried to wrap my mind around the fact that God was God just as much there as He was in America. Even though people did not know Him and I was an ocean away from all that was familiar, He was there. It was not that He had come with me across the ocean—He was already there, at work. He knew this new language and culture as well as He did mine. My view of God expanded through those walks. I thought of Psalm 139:9–10, "If I rise on the wings of the dawn, if I *settle on the far side of the sea*, even there your hand will guide me, your right hand will hold me fast" (emphasis added). There is nowhere I can go where He is not already there.

A family friend, Bob Tiede, told me that during one of the hardest transitions for his family, God kept bringing to mind the story of Jacob setting out from home after receiving his father's blessing. Jacob stopped for a night and had a dream in which God promised him (among other blessings) this: "*I am with you* and will watch over you wherever you go, and I will bring you back to this land. I will not leave you until I have done what I have promised you" (Genesis 28:15, emphasis added).

Sometimes this is all we have to cling to: God is with me and He will watch over me, and He will do what He promised in my life. If that were all, would that not be enough? When no one else might know who you are, where you are, what you are doing, when you have lost so much that is familiar and makes you feel solid, He is with you in that hidden place.

He is with you as you rock your baby to sleep. He is with you when you step into that new school. He is with you as you unpack those boxes, as you drive down unfamiliar streets. He is with you as you navigate a new role. He watches over you.

It is so easy to forget this truth. Verse 16 says, "When Jacob awoke from his sleep, he thought, 'Surely the Lord is in this place, and I was not aware of it.'"

Surely God is with us, but we are unaware. He wants us to abide in this holy truth—the God of the universe is closer than our own hearts wherever we are. Surely He has brought me to this place and abides with me here. This is good news. This is the place where I can rest from the storm.

Jacob continues by making a vow, "If God will be with me and will watch over me on this journey I am taking and will give me food to eat and clothes to wear so that I return safely to my father's household, then the LORD will be my God" (vv. 20–21).

Jacob made a choice to abide in the Lord. We are called to do the same. If it is true that God is with me in this place, then I will acknowledge His presence continually. I will let it be my lifeline when I am confronted with the hard, with loss, and with the mess of my own heart.

Stacey Thacker, author of *Hope for the Weary Mom*, felt this when she moved to Orlando, six weeks prior to her due date with her second child. In the weeks following the birth of her daughter, she confronted the intense loneliness of being unknown in a new place. One night, she brought this reality to the Lord at the grocery store: "What I really needed, I reminded him, was someone to say my name." [1]

As she pushed her cart down the aisle, she noticed two girls happily chatting, obviously good friends. Annoyed, she continued her shopping until one of them stopped her and said, "She wants to know if your name is Stacey."

It turned out Stacey went to school with one of those girls. How kind of God to answer her prayer in such a timely and specific way, and a precious reminder that He is always with us.

Who Is This God Who Abides with Me?

At an event I heard Dr. Bill Bright, founder of Campus Crusade for Christ, say, "Your view of God will determine your view of yourself and the world around you." It is important to not only acknowledge God's presence with us, but to continually remind ourselves who *is* this God who walks with us through transition.

One of the most powerful and comforting names of God is *El Roi*. We find this in Genesis when Hagar, a servant to Sarah and Abraham, is rejected by her mistress and sent away into the wilderness. An angel of God finds her by a spring and sends her back with the promise that God will multiply her offspring. "So [Hagar] called the name of the LORD who spoke to her, 'You are a God of seeing,' for she said, 'Truly here I have seen him who looks after me.' Therefore the well was called Beer-lahai-roi" (Genesis 16:13–14 ESV).

A Hebrew word, *El Roi* means "You are a God of seeing." And *Beer-lahai-roi* means "Well of the Living One who sees me."

El Roi, the God Who Sees. Not only is He with you, He sees everything about you. He sees your heart. He sees how this transition is affecting you—every tear, every joy, every frustrating moment, and every new discovery.

When I was a new mom, I remember marveling at this truth. During all those nighttime feedings, the endless days of feeding and changing and entertaining toddlers, He saw me. It all mattered to Him, even if no one else saw it. When I moved to the States with no ministry role waiting for me, I felt invisible to all but Him. He reminded me again and again, "I see you, Gina."

He might be the only One who knows what we are going through and who truly sees us, but we can find that He is enough.

El Roi sees our hearts, what we are going through, and He is compassionate toward us.

God has revealed other character traits to me in our various transitions. Our move to Singapore came a little bit out of left field. Leading up to it, I had a sense that change was coming but I thought it meant moving back to the States. I started having random thoughts like, "If we were to leave, what would I wish I had done?"

I made a list and started checking things off, doing all those tourist activities you forget to do when you actually live somewhere instead of visiting it. I took pictures of the ordinary objects around our neighborhood. Then came the invitation to move to Singapore and I wondered if those thoughts weren't so random after all.

The complicated logistics of moving our belongings to another country went more smoothly than we could imagine. We arrived in Singapore only hours after our friends had obtained the keys to the apartment they'd found for us. The next morning, we sat in our empty dining room, having had no word from our moving company (had our belongings made it?) and prayed that we would hear soon.

> El Roi sees our hearts, what we are going through, and He is compassionate toward us.

Five minutes later the doorbell rang. It was the movers. Within five hours, thanks to the decision to go with full-service packers, all our belongings were unpacked. It looked like we'd lived there for years, if we were the kind of people who never paint or hang art (we are not).

As I navigated that transition and witnessed God working out all the little details so well, I felt His tenderness. It was like He said, "Gina, I know how hard this is for you to move to a place you didn't choose. Let me make this easy on you."

When we moved again, the process was not nearly as smooth. We couldn't settle on a mover. Our visas were a mess. Our apartment was not ready. I reminded God that He had been so tender during the previous move. Why not this one? Because, He explained to me, it was not what I needed.

In moving to Singapore, I was full of trepidation and hesitation. It was not a move I wanted to make. Moving back, on the other hand, was a dream come true. We could not wait to move. In that transition, God called me to look to Him as provider. He called me to wait, to trust. Was He the same God who led us to Singapore? Was He still tender? Yes, but He chose to reveal another aspect of His character.

We need spiritual eyes to see not only who God is all the time but to also see how He reveals himself in each transition. Last spring, our daughter had to write a paper for an English assignment outlining how she had seen God at work in her life in the past year. At first she balked, unable to see what God had been doing. But as we talked through different areas of her life, she saw how He provided for her in this new place in unexpected ways. When she finished, she said, "I think I should look back at this to remind myself how God is faithful to me so I'll know I can trust Him in the future." Indeed.

When we begin with looking at who God is, it changes everything. As Dr. Bright said, it determines how we view ourselves and our circumstances. He does not change regardless of how our lives have shifted. The One who sees us is always revealing more of himself to us if we open our eyes to see.

RAISING OUR EBENEZERS

When God moved on behalf of His people in the Old Testament, stones were placed at significant locations as a memorial, a remembrance of who He is and what He had done. We see this in stories like Jacob and Laban meeting in Genesis 31, Joshua and the Israelites crossing the Jordan in Joshua 4, then reaching the promised land in Joshua 24, and Samuel leading the Israelites to victory in 1 Samuel 7.

Samuel calls the stone reminders *Ebenezer*, which means "God helps." From this we have the lyric by hymn writer Robert Robinson, "Here I raise mine Ebenezer, hither by Thy help I'm come." When we name who God is and how He has walked with us through transition, we raise our Ebenezer, our declaration that God is our unchanging rock.

Asking ourselves how God is revealing himself to us in transition turns our eyes upward, away from all that feels uncertain, all that is shifting. It has been helpful for me at times to sit for a moment and simply reflect on how I am experiencing God in times of turbulence.

I mentioned earlier that our son was distraught about our move to America. We left what felt like an idyllic situation where daily, he and his sister played with friends who were so close they felt like family. There were several nights after we moved when he cried himself to sleep, wondering if he would ever have that kind of connection again.

> When we name who God is and how He has walked with us through transition, we raise our Ebenezer, our declaration that God is our unchanging rock.

But over time, God provided. It took a while, but soon enough he felt like a part of a group again. By the time he graduated from high school, he had an enviable squad of close friends, guys and girls, who understood and loved him well.

On the night before he left for college, as he looked ahead to another new season, he told me, "I don't know how I'll find such a great group of friends again."

I reminded him of how he felt when we first moved here, how fearful and sad he was, and yet God provided abundantly. We talked about how the God who provided in the last season is the same God who provides in this season. And He is the God who goes ahead of us to the next one. He may not provide in the same way, but He will care for us, and that is the firm ground we stand on. Recounting His faithfulness season to season turns our eyes expectantly toward Him with confidence that He will work again.

Last fall, in response to walking through the start of a new school year and a trying season of leadership in our ministry, I wrote this: "Where can I abide in God today? He is with me. He is for me. He loves me. He delights in me. He provides. He guides. He knows me. He satisfies me. He is the God who sees. He will never leave me or forsake me. He knows the plans He has for me. He holds my heart. He has compassion for me. He is my rock of refuge. He is my shelter, my safe place. I can trust my heart to Him. He is faithful. He is good. He is my anchor."

In writing this, I felt my soul relax into the truth of who He is and how He reveals himself to me. It does our hearts good to remember how we see God's character at work in each season of our lives.

ABIDING IN WHO HE SAYS WE ARE

It is so easy to lose touch with our position as beloved children. We forget that what defines us, more than how well we are known or needed by anyone else, is that we are His.

If anyone were to ask us, "Do you know that your deepest value lies in being God's child?" I imagine most of us would agree. But do we really know this truth at heart level?

In Brennan Manning's book *Abba's Child*, a story is told of an Irish priest who travels back to Ireland to visit his elderly uncle. They took a walk together and the uncle began skipping. His nephew commented that he seemed very happy.

"Oh yes, lad, I am."
"May I ask why?"
"Oh yes. You see, my Abba is very fond of me." [2]

Our Abba is very fond of us. We are His. His love for us knows no end. He wants to be our rock, our refuge. Brennan Manning says, "Define yourself radically as one beloved by God."

This is echoed in Isaiah 43:1–2: "But now, this is what the LORD says—he who created you, Jacob, he who formed you, Israel: 'Do not fear, for I have redeemed you; I have summoned you by name; *you are mine*'" (emphasis added).

When we feel stripped of all the names, roles, titles, and responsibilities that defined us in the last season, when we're looking for who we are again, we must let this be the truth that defines us: we are His. We need to become practiced at listening to His voice telling us who we are when we feel the temptation to look to everyone else around us instead.

This was the lesson God taught me throughout most of our time in Singapore. The move there brought a significant change to my circumstances so that I no longer had time to be involved in ministry outside the home. I was known at the office only as "Erik's wife." I felt like I had lost who I was and didn't know how to find myself again.

We found connection in a small group at church, a wonderful oasis in the midst of our transition. Each of the eight couples in the group had also moved to Singapore within the same time frame. Our kids (and between us we had lots of them) were all relatively the same age. It became a lifeline for all of us.

But in that group, I felt insecure. I had spent my adult life with people who either worked in the same ministry as me, or with people to whom I was ministering. This small group was filled with people who were different from me in many ways. Not only were they different, it seemed like they were better versions of me. Better moms, better homeschoolers, better at life. I would walk away from times with our group thinking, "Who am I? What do I offer these people?" I was desperate for a solid identity.

That's when God started reminding me that I already had one. My circumstances might have changed, but who I am did not. For months, I read books about my identity in Christ. I read so many, in fact, that I started what I called my "Beloved journal." In it, I wrote down every quote, every verse, that reminded me who I am in Christ. Whenever I felt doubt or insecurity creep in, I grabbed that journal, laid on my bed, and read it over and over. As I did, I told myself, "this is who you are . . . this is who you are."

Over time, something happened. I began to feel solid inside. I began to define myself internally as His child. I found I was less self-conscious when I was with others because I wasn't looking to them to define me. Who He says I am became my abiding place.

Sarah Bessey puts it well in her book *Jesus Feminist*: "Living loved, we relax our expectations, our efforts, our striving, our rules, our spine, our breath, our plans, our job descriptions and checklist; we step off the treadmill of the world and the treadmill of religious performance. We are not the authors of our redemption. No, God is at work, and his love for us is boundless and deep, wide and high, beyond all comprehension. He remains faithful." [3]

I wish I could say that never changes, that I never doubt my worth. I so easily drift from that truth. But when I begin to feel unsettled again, I go back to those words and let them remind me of His love for me, how much I am valued by Him, that I am His. We cannot let anything else define us because everything else can change. But this never does.

One of the by-products of moving so often is that the concept of home becomes more nebulous. It both awakens in us a deep desire to feel at home and reminds us that our sense of home can be fleeting. Our versions of home here, as blissful as they might be, pale in comparison to being at home in God. He simultaneously brings to the surface our desire for home and invites us to find the satisfaction of that desire in Him. As C. S. Lewis said, "Our Father refreshes us on the journey with some pleasant inns, but will not encourage us to mistake them for home." [4] This is where we call home: who He is and who He says I am.

As we look at the hard aspects of transition, God calls us to anchor ourselves in His goodness. So much of the difficulty in this is the tension between God's truth and our own desires. And so much of what is hard revolves around the losses we incur. Thankfully, though what we lose is temporal, what we can rest in is unchanging. Tied to those losses, though, are real desires, and they are what we must face next.

CHAPTER FIVE

Navigating Desire

I HATE MESSES. I CAN TOLERATE THEM FOR A while, but then something in me snaps and I go into a flurry of cleaning. I have even, at times, thought I would enjoy being a cleaning lady for someone. I find great satisfaction in tidy, sanitized spaces.

During transitions, my heart often feels like a mess. I look around at the loose ends, the unmet desires, the raw emotions, and I don't know how to tidy them up. The hard, the losses—they raise emotions that unravel me. When we moved back to the U.S. I felt like God came into my heart and stirred things up, opened doors, pulled back the covers, and generally left everything in disarray. I was left standing in the middle of it, looking around at the chaos thinking, "That's the last time I invite that guy over."

The mess had a lot to do with seeing deeper levels of my own depravity, the ways I chase after life apart from God. Rather than letting myself acknowledge the hard, I sought ways to medicate or distract or numb myself. It was an emotional tangle of grief and excitement, loss and gain.

As uncomfortable as it was, the mess taught me that what satisfied my heart in the shallow end of the pool doesn't work well when God picks me up and throws me in deeper waters. Part of the issue is that while I know that God deeply loves and accepts my mess, I don't. In transition, this reality comes into sharp focus. And aiming for a quick fix—like telling myself that God loves me and I should just move on already—won't cut it. To do so would be like shoving all the mess in a closet and shutting the door.

So what do we do with the mess? I kept asking God that. And He kept saying, "Wait." This is what we most often do not want to do, but this is where we need to linger. God invites us to stay in the hard and loss long enough to begin to understand it, to name the parts that are being stirred in us, to take a good look at what's behind it, and why we do what we do.

It's here that we are confronted with desire.

There's a good reason many of us don't want to acknowledge the desires associated with transition. They can be intense, overwhelming, frightening even. Desire is a wily creature. It has gained a negative reputation in the Christian world. We fear being led astray by desire, being deceived by it. We associate it with lust and excess. It shows up in unexpected places and catches us off guard. And it always seems to take more time and energy to process than we'd like.

What do we do, then, with a verse like Psalm 37:4, "Take delight in the LORD, and he will give you the desires of your heart"? Or Psalm 21:2, "You have granted him his heart's desire"? Could it be that God does not look on our desire with so much contempt? Could it be that there is something good about our desire? It is time to redeem it.

When I say "desire," I don't mean "I want bacon" or "I long for a tropical vacation." I'm talking about deep heart desire— the desires we don't realize we have until we're confronted with loss. I'm talking about the desire to be liked, valued, respected, needed, important, powerful, competent, and noticed. If I do not get bacon on any given day, I am not going to be hurt. I won't experience pain if I don't get chocolate, though I may be a little disappointed. But if my desire to be valued goes unmet, there is potential for deep ache.

Transition reveals what we desire deepest in our hearts. It tells us what we want most.

How I responded to that bike guard revealed my deep desire to feel competent. That was probably more important to me than anything else in the moment. The loss I felt in stepping back from ministry certainly showed me how much I long to feel valuable and recognized for what I can do. The deeper we move into our hearts, the more our desires rise to the surface. And when they do, we have two main responses.

DEMANDING DESIRE

The first response is to demand for our desires to be met. We take matters into our own hands and seek the fulfillment of a desire on our own strength. We do this in several different ways.

For example, we may respond with anger. The pain of unmet desire often causes us to lash out. Our kids disobey, and we insist that they change. We yell and lay down the law and demand that they do what we ask. Why? Because at a deep heart level, we don't feel respected by them, and we hate that. Their disobedience feels dismissive to who we are and the work we do as parents.

Anger makes us feel strong, bigger than the pain of the unmet longing. In transition, this can look like impatience. Our words get shorter. Minor incidents bother us more than they would normally. We are quicker to respond with a harsh word or sarcasm. We are less likely to give grace.

On the surface, we blame the moving company for running late, or the map app that just sent us down the wrong road in a new city. But underneath, the anger is a symptom of unmet desire. And when something feels threatened, it is easier to make ourselves big with anger than to feel the fear, confusion, and frustration.

Another familiar route for demanding our desires be met is escape. Through escape, we try to meet our own desires by opting out of the frustrating reality and settling for a false substitute. As my friend, Missy, put it when I commented on her well-decorated home shortly after she'd moved to our city, "I self-medicated with Home Goods."

We self-medicate our desire through Netflix, shopping, fantasy, food, social media—anything to take our mind away from the ache we feel from unmet needs. Escape can be an external distraction with something like alcohol or television, or a much subtler and hidden escape to a place in our minds.

Sometimes, the escape is back to a place or position we left, at least mentally. We can idealize it and long for it, much like the Israelites longed to return to Egypt when the way to the promised land proved challenging. It might simply be escaping to a place in our minds where we feel in control, happy, satisfied—whatever it is that we don't currently feel. When we do this, we steal energy needed to live the life we're actually in.

The demand for desire to be satisfied can manifest in control. When I was little, I was a big fan of the Little Miss books, so I was happy when someone tapped into this market and started making Little Miss T-shirts. The first one I bought was Little Miss Sunshine. I bought it somewhat ironically, or maybe just by faith, because I am not always the most cheerful person on the block.

I also bought Little Miss Bossy, which is more my reality. What I need most when in transition is a shirt that says, "Little Miss Control Freak." People should have fair warning. I do not like the fact that I try so hard to control my world. I used to say I was a recovering controlaholic because I have learned ways to unclench, but God has made it clear to me that at a deeper level in me, the desire to control is still alive and well—and transitions bring it to the surface.

In transition, we control by sticking harder to routines. We find safety in our own habits. We insist on doing things our way, keeping the kids closer, and participating in activities we know we can do well which, in new situations, often translates to "not many." So our worlds grow smaller because if we cannot have what we truly want, we will make sure we get what we can control.

Anne Lamott says, "It helps to resign as the controller of your fate. All that energy we expend keeping things running right is not what keeps things running right." [1] None of the ways we demand a desire be met ever truly satisfies us at a heart level, and ultimately, they are a faulty attempt to self-protect and self-rely without trusting God.

> None of the ways we demand a desire to be met ever truly satisfies us at a heart level, and ultimately, they are a faulty attempt to self-protect and self-rely without trusting God.

DEADENING DESIRE

We could go the opposite direction and kill our desire. Instead of demanding that our desire be satisfied, we dismiss it. We convince ourselves that it's selfish to want it in the first place, that it's really not that important anyway, and that we better suck it up and deal with life. Or we simply pretend it doesn't exist. Killing desire manifests itself in a number of ways.

The easiest is to ignore it—just don't question what's happening. In transition, this is nearly effortless. We stay busy, we don't reflect, we don't examine. We get lost in setting up a new house, learning the new job, figuring out this parenting gig, and moving on. If we can keep focused on the surface activity, we can skirt the emotions that are trying to bubble up.

If ignoring our desire doesn't work, we try to numb it. Some of us do realize that something's amiss, but rather than face what is being stirred, we shut it down and pretend that everything is fine, which I've often heard stands for Feelings Inside Not Expressed. I have seen people become so practiced at numbing their own emotions that when they try to ask themselves what they feel, they have no idea. They have learned to dissociate from their hearts.

But maybe we cannot numb ourselves enough. Well then, at least we can minimize our problems. We try to look on the bright side, hold back complaints, and convince ourselves that we're being selfish. In many ways, it makes sense. It even helps for a little while, protecting us from pain. But it is dishonest, and it keeps us from truly making peace with change.

When we cannot minimize within ourselves, we have comparison to help us out. We feel we have no right to consider our situation difficult when compared to the pain and challenges others are facing. Looking at someone else's struggle, we think, *Oh, but it could be so much worse*, or, *At least I don't have that to deal with.* And in effect, we shut the lid on our hearts.

Brené Brown, in her book *I Thought It Was Just Me (But It Isn't)*, says, "*At least* is not a good lead-in for an empathetic response." It is often simply a way to shut down desire. [2]

With a Christian twist, minimizing takes on the form of spiritualizing. We tell ourselves we just need to have faith and we will get through it, that all things work together for good. We say, "God's gonna get me through this," or, "It's where God wants us." All that is true, so true. But it does not help us face what we are feeling and deal with it in a healthy way. At the worst, people use it as an opportunity to shame themselves because it carries the wounding message: I just don't have enough faith. I'm not trusting Him enough.

Sadly, deadening our hearts feels like the "Christian" option. We justify it, thinking, *I'm denying myself and taking up my cross.* But denying ourselves and killing desire are not the same thing. Taking up our cross involves acknowledging our desire and making the intentional choice to put it in God's hands, committing to follow Him with that desire open and unmet. Killing desire closes down our hearts and denies the opportunity for God to work in them. It is self-protection, not surrender.

Take the example of a new mom: she is exhausted, confused, doubtful of herself, lonely. Those are all valid emotions to be experiencing in this new stage of life. She probably wants nothing more than to have a day when she feels normal, competent, refreshed, known. It is important for her to have those needs met, yet the demands of motherhood do not always allow for it exactly when she needs it.

To deny herself and take up her cross would be to go to God with all those desires and say honestly, "This is hard. I don't know what I'm doing. I'm tired and lonely. I need you. Help me to keep going."

She acknowledges the hard, owns her losses, calls out her desires. She lays them out before God, as it says in Psalm 38:9, "All my longings lie open before you, Lord; my sighing is not hidden from you." In this place of honesty and reliance on God, she continues with her calling as a mom.

The other option is for her to keep silent, press on, and deny those desires. In doing so she misses an opportunity to connect with God and to be vulnerable with others about how this transition is impacting her. Her heart closes a little more.

Treating ourselves and our hearts in this way speaks of contempt against ourselves and others. In *The Wounded Heart*, Dan Allender writes, "Contempt is a cruel anesthetic to longing. As long as I turn my condemnation against myself, I block the potential of your movement toward me and my longing for you to care. When I turn my condemnation against you, I am free from believing that I want anything from you. In either case, contempt kills longing." [3]

When we deaden desire, we cannot embrace change and bring our whole hearts through the process of transition. My friend Bruce Edstrom says, "Contempt and shame seal within the heart that which deadens and cuts off all that has capacity to be alive, the giving and receiving of love and ardent affection."

The danger here is that how we respond to our own hearts in transition will set a pattern for how we respond to others as well.

Years ago, I became familiar with a personality typing system called the Enneagram. It is based on the idea that there are nine types of people, and each type is driven by a particular root desire. For example, we might be motivated by the desire to be good, or to be needed, to be successful, competent, strong, or safe. Others are motivated by the desire to be at peace, or to feel that they are special and offer something unique to the world. As we recognize those desires within us, we can begin to see where we are seeking our own fulfillment. Are we looking to God to satisfy us, or are we trying to satisfy desires in our own way?

Our move back to the States made these desires come to the surface for me. Things that I could normally ignore were suddenly in my face. I felt raw, exposed. Many of those desires felt more acute for the simple reason that they had been so well met in my previous situation, and now they were counted among my losses in this new place. In moving here, I desperately desired to be known, seen, needed, valuable. I wanted the approval of others. I wanted to be seen as impressive. I wanted to be recognized.

> How we respond to our own hearts in transition will set a pattern for how we respond to others as well.

For a long time, I shunned these desires. I had contempt for them. I didn't want it to be true that I longed for those things so much.

But though the way I pursue those desires may be wrong, the desires themselves are not. What is wrong about desire is seeking its fulfillment in things other than God. When we do that, our desires become idols.

I can easily make longing to feel valuable an idol. I will posture myself in such a way that people see my best qualities, that they see what I can do. I often feel like I am on the school playground waiting to be picked, waiting for someone to say, "Hey, that girl. We need her on our team!" And if you pick me, that same desire to be valuable can drive me to aim for MVP status.

What if I did something different with this desire? What if I went to God and listened to His voice telling me that I am already valuable to Him? All of these desires we have are met in Him. He gives them to us so that we will feel our need for Him. And He satisfies my need to feel valuable in a way that no one else could ever do. Why? Because His value for me doesn't change with my circumstances.

When we acknowledge the truth of the emotions raised by our losses, it opens the door for God to meet us in our pain. I am not saying we should dwell on our problems; on the contrary, it takes great faith to choose joy in the midst of the challenges. However, true joy involves honestly acknowledging the challenges and losses, and still choosing it—not pretending it is not as hard as it is.

In this way, transition becomes a gift. The veil is pulled back and we can see what we are doing with our hearts. The places where we feel the greatest losses are the places where we have the deepest desires. Are we asking God to speak into those desires? Or are we looking to the world and to our own ways to meet them in illegitimate and, ultimately, unsatisfying ways?

God created us with deep heart-level needs and desires. He created them so that we will seek Him. Unfortunately, many of us, when confronted with our own desires, have contempt for them. We do not live in a world where we are encouraged to want.

DESIRE IN SCRIPTURE

When I look at the Bible, I am encouraged because we see there that Jesus affirmed desire. You never see Him shut it down. On the contrary, you see Him asking people, "What do you want?"

In Matthew 20:29–34, He poses this question to two blind men who respond with, "We want our sight." In Mark 10:35–45, the disciples James and John ask to be seated at His right and left (a pretty gutsy request). In John 1:35–42, He asks the first disciples who are following Him, and their indirect response is that they simply want to be with Him.

In each case, Jesus does not condemn their desire. Rather, He responds by giving them what they need. God already knows what we want. In the midst of upheaval in our lives, He sees what is stirred in us even more than we do. He is calling us to name it, to bring it into the light, and deal with it. He wants us to bring our desire to Him and rest in Him for the satisfaction of it. Stop responding to it in heart-hardening or heart-wandering ways. Let Him speak to it.

In the story of the prodigal son in Luke 15:11–32, we find a perfect example of these two harmful responses to desire. The younger son took his desire for more and ran off to demand the world meet it: "The younger son got together all he had, set off for a distant country and there squandered his wealth in wild living" (v. 13). He escaped into his own methods of satisfying desire.

The older son deadened his desire: "The older brother became angry and refused to go in" (v. 28). He shut down his heart and separated himself from his father, his brother.

And then there is the father who waits in love for his young son to come home, the father who loves his older son enough to go out and find him. He aches with the desire to be in relationship with his sons. In doing so, he brought his whole heart. This is the example God sets for us.

Bringing Desires to Light

I have had my share of experiences with desire in transitions, but there was one in particular that God used to change the way I respond to my heart's longings.

In the fall of 2012, my family prayed for a dog. We went to a local alley full of small stores that sold mostly fish and birds, but also had a pet supply store. By faith, we bought what we would need for a puppy—food, a leash, a crate, toys. It was challenging to find puppies in that part of the world that were healthy and immunized. As we walked down the alley full of shops, Erik prayed out loud, "God, would you give us a puppy?"

Moments later, out of a fish store wandered a small brown-and-black dog. She was the last of her litter, her mother being the pet of the store owner. Five minutes and $9 later, we were dog owners. God had answered our prayers, and several months of unexpected spiritual transformation began in my life.

Scout was six weeks old and unimmunized when we brought her home. Many dogs in Asia carry disease, so our vet advised us not to take her outside for nine weeks until she had received all her shots. We lived on the twelfth floor of our apartment building where I homeschooled our two children. Shortly after, Erik left on a business trip for nearly two weeks. The conditions were perfect for my transformation (I keep calling it transformation, which sounds better than "my own private hell").

In my efforts to train this puppy, I decided the kids were old enough to "homeschool" themselves. (They were nine and eleven and, in case you're wondering, I was wrong.) I spent my days yelling up the stairs for them to quit fighting and do their work, while I watched our puppy have accidents all over the living room floor.

As the weeks passed, I became more and more angry. I was angry at the kids for not doing what they were incapable of doing. I was angry with the puppy for not getting with my training program. I was angry with my husband for leaving me with this mess. I was angry with myself for not being able to get on top of the mess.

I was bumping up against desire.

It was the desire to be a good mother, to be a competent dog trainer, to enjoy this new season. I was ashamed to admit that I was not thrilled about our new family member, so I did not talk about it. People would see her and say, "She's so cute! Don't you just love her?" And truth be told: she is the cutest dog I have ever seen, in my unbiased opinion. But how could I answer that then? What kind of coldhearted person was I to not love this sweet puppy? We were living out the cliché that the kids want the dog and Mom takes care of it.

God used that transition of becoming a dog owner to help me see clearly how I was dealing with desire. You wouldn't think something so cute and lovable could be the crucible for my spiritual growth, but she was. In fact, after several months in this new role, God stirred so much up in me that I literally had to go to counseling to wrestle through it all. A dog made me go to counseling. How many people can say that?

My counselor encouraged me to listen to my own heart when I found myself becoming angry. What was it showing me? I saw that I wanted to be a good mom, but I told myself that I shouldn't look to my kids to tell me my worth. I wanted to conquer this dog-training situation; I told myself to just bear with it. Seeing my desire didn't seem to be helping.

Months later, I chatted with my family on Skype and mentioned offhandedly that I was not the biggest fan of our dog. Not realizing the depth of my frustration, they lightheartedly responded with comments like, "What? How can you not like her? You know you're talking to dog lovers here!" In my heart, my response was, "See? It was right for you to be ashamed of this. Good thing you didn't tell anyone else."

After we hung up, I asked God how it could have gone differently and in response, He asked what I wished I had heard from them instead.

I wished they had empathized with how hard it was to train such a young puppy in our situation, how they understood all that I was trying to do, that they would feel the same way.

"Then say that to yourself," He said.

So I did. I talked to myself about how hard it must be to train a too-young puppy on the twelfth floor of an apartment building. I empathized with myself about the strain of juggling single parenting, dog training, and homeschooling. That takes a lot out of a person. I told myself it was okay to not love it. Or her.

This was what I had been missing. I could see my desire, but I poured contempt on it. I wanted to not want it so much. But after that, I began to respond to my desire as a trusted friend would. When I saw that desire to be a good mom, I said to myself, "Of course you want to be a good mom," or to my dislike of my new role as dog owner, "It must be a difficult thing to do on the twelfth floor."

Transition gives us an opportunity to respond to our hearts differently. We can see our messy, longing hearts for what they are, and say, "Of course you feel that way. It's normal. You're normal. Now let's take this to God."

We can say this confidently and compassionately because that is what God would say to us. He has compassion on our mess, on our desire. He gave it to us and He wants us to be satisfied in Him. In the middle of transition, we can hear Him say, "I'm sorry it's hard. I see your losses. I know your desire. Come to me. Rest in me."

The more we see the compassion God has for us, for everyone, the more we extend it to ourselves, the more it naturally overflows to others.

We must speak to ourselves as God speaks to us.

When we withhold compassion from ourselves, it doesn't reserve more for others.

It just causes us to live with a scarcity mind-set. But the more we see the compassion God has for us, for everyone, the more we extend it to ourselves, the more it naturally overflows to others.

HONORING OUR HEARTS

Part of navigating transition well is giving space for the desires in our hearts to be what they are, and, more than that, to call them okay, normal, right, valid, true. When we call our emotions valid and tell ourselves it is alright to feel what we are feeling, however negative or messy it might be, we honor our hearts. This develops a measure of compassion for ourselves that will naturally spill over toward others, because we are responding to ourselves as God does.

When the desire of mine to be valuable reared its head when we returned to the U.S., I'll admit I was not ready to honor it. Sometimes, it was so strong it felt like a physical ache. I told myself I just needed to rest in God's value of me, that it was wrong for me to look to others to tell me what I'm worth. That is true, but that reasoning also enabled me to shut down my desire.

In the end, God kept encouraging me to just sit with it. I want to feel valuable. Many of us do. We are valuable in His eyes, but sometimes the world won't affirm it, particularly not in new places or situations where our value goes unseen.

What are the desires that are raised in you during transition? How do you respond to them? Can you name them and let them be?

In her book *Strong Women, Soft Hearts*, Paula Reinhart writes, "What will you do with your heart, even if no one understands or offers validation? Will you honor your heart with the dignity God does—regardless of how you are met by others?"[4]

We are often alone in transition. Though we may have relationships where we can share our true hearts, even the people who love us most don't always understand the changes we are experiencing. Other people may not give us the emotional space to process and validate the emotions we feel. Process and validate them anyway. Your heart is on its own timeline.

For the first few months back in the U.S., I felt like people gave me space to be a bit of a mess. After all, most people could recognize that we'd just been through a tough move. Soon though, the question popped up: "Are you settled yet?" It was an innocent question, but intended or not, what it implied was, "You should probably be feeling okay by now." I wasn't.

Over time, the awareness others have of your transition will diminish (if it was ever there at all). When that happens, it can cause you to feel like you should be over it, like you should be back to feeling normal. Maybe you do, but maybe you don't and that's okay.

Honoring your heart is about giving yourself grace with not being okay, even when no one else does. It's agreeing with God that your feelings are normal.

Know this: God does not despise your desire. He created it and He welcomes it. He is uncovering a deep hunger for Him at your very core. He wants you to see that desire and let it lead you to Him. Embrace it, bring it to Jesus. Trust that He is stirring it up for a reason, drawing your heart closer to Him, and leading you to drink deeply from His well of life-giving water.

Bring Desire on the Journey

In the 2012 movie about addiction entitled *Thanks for Sharing*, one of the characters says, "Emotions are like children. You don't let them drive the car, but you can't put them in trunk." [5]

So true. Then what do we do with the wily kids?

Well, you let them be kids. They stay in the car with you. Sometimes they get a little annoying and tiring, but they're just being who they are. They're along for the journey.

So is desire. It's part of the journey. We don't want to let our desires drive us, but we can't stuff them away like they don't exist. So what do we do with desire?

We sit with it. We sit with it like the father did in the story of the prodigal son, knowing that in doing so we bring our whole hearts into the journey. We incline our desires toward Him for their satisfaction instead of our own human ways. And we honor the natural, God-given desires we have, so that in seeing them, we can develop a compassion for ourselves that mirrors God's compassion for us.

Our challenge is to be like Jesus, to go before God with our whole hearts. Not hearts that are ignorant or blind to the difficulties of life, but hearts that believe God is stirring these desires in us for good purposes.

In transition, we are given the opportunity to look to Him for our deepest heart needs. Whatever desires are raised for us in times of transitions, they were made to be acknowledged. Instead of shutting our desires up in a box, we need to lay them open and bare before God, asking Him to sift them. We ask Him to show us how to hold them, how to respond to them in ways that honor our hearts and reflect His grace and love.

Sitting with desire is a challenge. It brings us to corners of our heart where we feel the extent of our deep, human need. And rightly so, because it calls us to anchor ourselves in His strength instead of our own.

CHAPTER SIX

Anchored in His Strength

AFTER SEVERAL YEARS LIVING OVERSEAS, I WAS IN a sweet spot. Our kids were two and four years old, and I felt like I was finally getting a handle on this whole "mommy" thing. My language skills were decent (meaning, I no longer had to use sign language to communicate my thoughts. Hallelujah). I was doing ministry work that I loved with women who were as much of a blessing to me as I was trying to be to them. One day, I thought to myself, "I *love* my life."

My very next thought was, "Something's going to change."

I had that thought, not because I figured God was out to spoil my fun, but because I had been studying Deuteronomy. These verses stuck out to me: "And when the LORD your God brings you into the land . . . with great and good cities that you did not build, and houses full of all good things that you did not fill, and cisterns that you did not dig, and vineyards and olive trees that you did not plant—and when you eat and are full, then take care lest you forget the LORD" (Deuteronomy 6:10–12 ESV).

I knew those verses were true of me. I was in a place where I was comfortable, I did not feel like I *needed* God. I was in danger of forgetting Him. So God saw fit to move us to Singapore, where . . . well, I felt my need.

God uses transition to bring us to places of deeper reliance on Him. Rather than depending on our own means to satisfy our desires, we come to rest in His strength. He is the rock of refuge where our hearts can find rest in the midst of a needy journey. But in order to rest, we must embrace our neediness.

No one likes being in a place where we feel weak or needy. Our society places a premium on self-reliance and self-sufficiency. It's practically what our country was built on. The word "needy" invokes images of that desperately imbalanced person we hope to avoid at church, the one whose tears are just a little too close to the surface, the one who traps you against the wall with her latest drama. None of us wants to be "that" person.

On the other hand, we all say we want to grow. We want to become more Christlike, more dependent on God. We just would rather not go through the pain it takes to get there. We want the kind of fairy-tale growth that comes with long prayer walks in the woods, after which we emerge deeper and more mature. Unfortunately, it doesn't work that way. Instead, God cultivates our growth through times of weakness, need, and humility. And transition is a powerful catalyst to those places.

Bringing Us to a Place of Need

Our natural response to our weakness is never to admit our need or look to Him for strength. More often, we respond as though God is testing our mettle. We come to think that the goal is to develop our own strength. And sure, after a few of these transition rodeos, we do learn how to weather them better. We become adept at picking ourselves up, pressing forward, and holding it together. We might even impress others with our ability to roll with the punches.

We are often told, "God won't give you more than you can handle." Friends, that phrase is not found in Scripture. I understand what people are trying to say—we know that God will get us through whatever challenges we're facing. Besides the fact that it's a misinterpretation of 1 Corinthians 10:13, the problem with this phrase is that it puts the impetus on *us* to get through it. This false promise leads us to believe that it is up to us to scrounge around and find the strength to weather whatever challenge we ourselves are facing. If we don't, our inability to handle it means either we failed, or God did. Both are false.

One of our coworkers suffered a waterskiing injury that required surgery to repair a disconnected muscle. The ordeal left him immobilized for eight weeks. He could do nothing but lie on his couch, dependent on others to do everything for him. Making the most of it, he asked people to come to his house for meetings usually held at the office. He made phone calls and continued to work. That is until one day when God told him, "I didn't put you on your back so that you could learn to work lying down."

God is not impressed with how well we can function in a given situation. His goal is not to make us stronger but to help us look around and see that we do not have what it takes.

As C. S. Lewis noted, "God has not been trying an experiment on my faith or love in order to find out their quality. He knew it already. It was I who didn't. In this trial He makes us occupy the dock, the witness box, and the bench all at once. He always knew that my temple was a house of cards. His only way of making me realize the fact was to knock it down." [1]

It is a gift to be brought to this place, where God knocks down our house of cards, where we are at the end of our resources. Beyond our resources, really. God doesn't take us to places of need so we can prove how strong we are; He takes us through them so we can discover greater depths of His strength.

God won't give us something we can't handle *with His help*.

All those needs that transition raises, the ones we talked about in the previous chapter—God wants to be our first resource for them. Over time, He is gracious to provide for those needs through other people, situations, and opportunities. In the meantime, this is our chance to see how deep His storehouses are.

At my lowest point in the transition to Singapore, when I had sat on the couch and prayed for God to make it easier, I was brought to a place of dependence. At the end of my resources, I couldn't homeschool, I couldn't keep my house in order, I couldn't drum up new friends for our kids to replace the abundance they had before, I couldn't be both parents in place of my traveling husband. I didn't have what I needed for life, at least not in myself. That season brought me to my knees, literally and spiritually.

And it was one of the greatest gifts God has ever given me.

Something that God kept bringing to mind during that season was the idea that He was leading me to places where I was lost enough to give up control and trust Him to lead me instead.

It's only when we are lost enough to let go of our feeble attempts to make life work, when we feel the reality of our smallness in the world, that we can grasp God's greatness in contrast.

God forbid we never come to the end of our resources, because if we don't, we never see how great God is and how much more He can do than we can. Second Corinthians 1:8–9 reads, "We were under great pressure, far beyond our ability to endure, so that we despaired of life itself. Indeed, we felt we had received the sentence of death. But this happened *that we might not rely on ourselves but on God*, who raises the dead" (emphasis added).

Most of us will probably not experience the kind of intense pressure that led Paul to write those words, but if we call transition hard, as we should, we know that there are times when we despair. Times when our hearts are too full of unmanageable emotion. Times when we feel stretched beyond our ability, when we've grown shockingly intimate with our desperate need, that we might not rely on ourselves, but on God.

> It's only when we are lost enough to let go of our feeble attempts to make life work, when we feel the reality of our smallness in the world, that we can grasp God's greatness in contrast.

LET HIM HELP YOU

When I became a homeschool mom, I entered it with a naïve pride. After all, Ethan was only five. How hard could it be to teach a kindergartner? Turns out it can be incredibly difficult if said kindergartner is not interested in learning.

Three months into this educational experiment, I collapsed into a chair in the corner of my bedroom to discuss the situation with

God. I prayed, "God, you are not going to believe this, but . . ." and told Him that I had no idea what I was doing. I was pretty sure I'd made some mistake that landed me in a place so far beyond what I thought I could manage.

Ever hear God chuckle? I'm pretty sure I did. Not in an unkind way, but in an, "Oh sweet child, I love you" kind of way. Appropriate, given the situation. And then He said, "Of course you don't know what you're doing. Let me *help you.*"

I admit that thought hadn't occurred to me. Sometimes it just doesn't. We are hardwired to go to our own resources first, and if those aren't sufficient, only then do we look to God. But relying on human resources will only enable us to accomplish human tasks. God calls us to bigger situations than that, situations for which our resources are simply not enough.

> **Relying on human resources will only enable us to accomplish human tasks.**

So I began acknowledging my weakness to God. Rather than pushing through a hard homeschool day, I let myself take a break to ask God for the patience and wisdom I needed. I stopped expecting myself to know what I was doing and owned my insufficiency before Him, trusting Him to guide me. Rather than feeling like a failure, I felt relief—the burden to figure out this new season wasn't on me. God was willing to carry me.

Depending on God in Scripture

When the Israelites left Egypt and made their way to the promised land, they left behind all they knew and ventured into the unknown. Along the way they found themselves in need. In Exodus 16, they faced hunger and God provided for them through daily manna. They quickly realized it was no good trying to store up for the next day—it spoiled. So every day for forty years, they relied on God to rain down bread from heaven to sustain them. This is a beautiful picture of the kind of dependence God calls us to in the midst of transition. Each day, we look to Him for what we need, knowing that it will be there.

God calls us to bring our needs before Him every day and receive His provision. It's not a strength we can store up for the long haul—we are to come day by day, moment by moment. To do this, we can't ignore the areas where transition makes us feel weak. Instead, we must bring them to the light so He can strengthen us with His power.

Depending on God is not simply a better option; it's an issue of obedience. The Old Testament is a cautionary tale to us who continue to strive to do life in our own strength. Over and over we see biblical characters turn away from the living God to rely on themselves and useless idols. In Jeremiah 2:13, God's attitude toward this is clear: "My people have committed two sins: They have forsaken me, the spring of living water, and have dug their own cisterns, broken cisterns that cannot hold water."

God doesn't just hope that we will rely on Him in transition because He has more to offer. He commands us to rely on Him because He is God. He is worthy of being our first resource. He is the only one who deserves that place in our lives. And through transition, He lets our neediness come to the surface, loosens our hold on our sinful ways of satisfying it, and returns us to the spring of living water. If we let go of our self-sufficiency, God can bring new life to us and to others, through us.

OUR ANCHOR IN THE STORM

As we prepared to move back to the U.S., I felt like I could see the coming storm. It was a tempest of tears, adjustment, goodbyes, new experiences, old memories. We were about to take our kids out of the country where they were born and grew up. We were leaving friends we had known for a decade. The impact would be great.

I was tempted to hide in the cellar while the storm passed, but I knew that would simply be an attempt to protect my heart. Instead, I pictured Erik and me manning a lifeboat together, pulling our children tight to us, and bracing against the winds, yelling, "Hold on, kids!" We had to stay together, knowing that to keep our hearts open for good, we must keep them open to all of life—including the painful parts. As one of my friends said, "The sorrow is so great because it's been so good."

Eventually we came to the point where it felt like the gale had passed, and we were faced with assessing the damage. How was our boat doing? Where were we now? How do we raise the sail and head in a new direction?

Transitions take us out of our comfort zones and into uncharted territory. It's tempting to feel that if we prepare well and stay on top of the details, we can weather the storm on our own. But we have to remember that the storm is bigger than we are—that even in the fiercest tempest, God is our refuge, our anchor, our safe place, and shelter. And more than that, He is the master of the storm. He knows the boundaries of it. He knows how much it will tear at us and stir up our hearts. We don't hide from the storm—we depend on Him to take us through it.

Even in the fiercest tempest, God is our refuge, our anchor, our safe place, and shelter. And more than that, He is the master of the storm.

STAY CLOSE TO THE SOURCE

A few years ago, my husband led a major organizational change in our ministry. On top of that, parenting our teens was a greater challenge that fall than we expected. I found I needed to hear God's voice more often. I had to go back to the well of His resources every day.

Isaiah 58:11 says, "The LORD will guide you always; he will satisfy your needs in a sun-scorched land and will strengthen your frame. You will be like a well-watered garden, like a spring whose waters never fail." I love the promise here, that He will water the dry ground of our souls.

I want the garden of my soul to be an easy one to tend. You know, the occasional watering, sun, and a little food. In times of change, though, our souls dry up more quickly. We become dry and desperate for His inpouring.

Dependence means to stay in constant awareness of our need, and to humbly go to Him more often than usual. Dependence looks like believing that no part of this transition is too small to go to Him for help. We don't need to carry any of this alone. He wants to be our source in it all.

The famous hymn reprise, "I need thee every hour," is never more true than in the midst of change. Every hour, sometimes every minute, we take our desperate prayers for help to His feet. It's tiring, this going back again and again. I want it to be easier, but I know that His way is better. So I have to go daily, hourly, moment by moment even, for what I need to sustain me in this season.

In hard times, God's resources are just as abundant as in easy times. He is glad to provide all we need to not only get through, but to thrive. Our job then is to humble ourselves, pick up our buckets, and go to the well, as often as it takes.

> Our job then is to humble ourselves, pick up our buckets, and go to the well, as often as it takes.

CHILDLIKE DEPENDENCE

To admit our needs is to be childlike. Children know they don't have it together. They don't even try. They freely tell you what they need and they are not ashamed of it. They don't expect to do life on their own. Jesus said let the children come to Him, because the kingdom of God belongs to them. Paula Reinhart, in *Strong Women, Soft Hearts*, reminds us, "Needs are not enemies to conquer, they are part of what keeps us returning to the Lord." [2]

We do not have to be afraid of our need. In times of change, we can embrace our weakness and let it lead us to God. Because, as John Ortberg wrote, "The unlimited neediness of the soul matches the unlimited grace of God." [3] There, in God's grace, we can rest our weary souls and know that He will be the strength we so desperately need.

I said in the previous chapter that God doesn't despise our need. Instead, He welcomes it. He longs to show His strength in our weakness. As we move through transition, we have to see the places where God is calling us to depend on Him. Instead of relying on the wisdom of the internet or the advice of others, we look to God to give us discernment and direction. We look to Him to provide for the financial, social, emotional, and logistical needs that arise in a new location. God calls for us to depend on Him to satisfy the desires in our hearts rather than seeking to satisfy them on our own.

When the transition is hard, we wave the white flag and say, "This is too much for me, God, and I need you in this." As we acknowledge our losses, we are reminded of the constant invitation to depend on His abundant strength and grace. And when we name our desires, they can lead us to find satisfaction in God.

C. S. Lewis said, "The thing is to rely on God. The time will come when you will regard all this misery as a small price to pay for having been brought to that dependence. Meanwhile, the trouble is that relying on God has to begin all over again every day as if nothing has yet been done."[4] In daily depending on God, our hearts will find true rest and peace. We can stop trying to be our own saviors and lean on the One who is our rock, our refuge, our anchor in the storm.

May He lead us to places where we are lost enough to let ourselves be led by the One who is wiser and stronger than we are. Together, let's place our hope in Him because He is the only source in life that will never change.

CHAPTER SEVEN

Navigating Expectations

BUYING A HOUSE IN THE STATES FROM 6,000 MILES away was a bit complicated. Four months before the big move, we spent a week touring houses for sale in the new neighborhood. Out of the fifteen that we saw, we chose one typical for the area. We call them "Disney subdivisions," new constructions where the colors stay a muted and limited range. Open-concept floors look out on the lanai and, if you are fortunate, a backyard pool will get you through the summer. The floor plans vary little, which makes it easy to find the bathroom in your neighbor's house. It feels like *The Truman Show*, like maybe each morning, everyone exits their driveways at the same time.

Despite the cookie-cutter view, I was excited. I could picture myself in the kitchen, watching our kids play with new friends in the pool. Our parents could stay over in the guest room downstairs, and the second-floor landing was perfect for homeschooling.

And then the offer looked sketchy, and we pulled out. The only other opportunity to see houses in person came a few weeks later, when Erik went back for a week. He told me he had found *the one*. I looked at pictures, and I *hated* it. It was as far from the Disney subdivision as you could get. A custom-built house, it looked like it had been designed by drunk people. You could see seven different colors of wall paint from the living room. It was dark. The kitchen didn't overlook the pool at all. And throughout the floor plan, there were design choices that made me ask, "Why? Why like this?"

Despite our reluctance to join the masses in the subdivisions, I had come to expect the airy openness and neutral color palette they offered. This house, on the other hand, was not what I expected at all.

Desire and expectations walk hand in hand. While desires speak to what we want, expectations go even further; they speak to what we strongly believe ought to be ours. Expectations are hopeful assumptions, "this is what my world should look like and this is how it should work." Expectations are desires with a defined shape. I would go so far as to say they feel like rights.

As Christians, we never say, "I deserve this" or "God owes me this," but we live that way functionally. At the least, many of our expectations overlap with legitimate needs. What complicates the situation is that we are unaware of our expectations and at the same time, unconsciously determine that they will be met.

We have expectations about how we spend our time, how much we will like this new stage in life, where we will find belonging. . . . We place expectations on ourselves, on others, and on our circumstances. Sometimes we enter new seasons with optimism, anticipation, and excitement only to find that things don't measure up the way we thought they would. Other times we move into transition with low expectations, guarding our hearts against disappointment. But a better path opens to us when we bring our expectations to the table.

EXPECTATIONS ON OURSELVES

I was pregnant with my firstborn when we moved overseas. The whole purpose of the move was to work for an organization that ministered to students and so I planned to keep working after our son arrived. In preparation, I made a schedule of how I thought I'd organize my time between work and caring for a newborn.

When Ethan was about three months old, I found that schedule and had a good laugh. There was no accounting for when he would eat or sleep. Apparently, I had expected to give birth to a Cabbage Patch doll that I could then set in a baby carrier and go on with my life as I had before.

In my new role as a mom, I assumed I would know what to do, or at least be able to figure it out quickly. I wanted to be a good mom and still have a life apart from taking care of my son. I expected to be able to exercise, maintain healthy habits, and get my body back. I expected to be able to do pretty much everything I did before, only with a little person in tow. My expectations were huge and unrealistic, and I was definitely disappointed that reality was not what I imagined.

All too easily, we internalize the world's expectations for us without even noticing it. From the cultural voices and messages that surround us, we form an unrealistic picture of how well we should be doing, what our homes should look like, and how our marriages and children should be. We try to make our lives match a fantasy picture of the perfect family. You know what I'm talking about—the family who takes a cross-country move in stride, who packs their house themselves while their kids play quietly with cardboard boxes because they're so wildly creative. They label everything like pros, so that week-old stack of unpacked boxes doesn't faze them because they know where everything is. They plug into their new community within days. They seem perfect. I would say I hate them but they don't exist. Still, we try to be them.

Unrealistic expectations drive many of us to push beyond the limits of our natural resources. They are a recipe for discouragement, especially when transition drains so many of those resources to begin with.

EXPECTATIONS ON OTHERS

We all carry expectations on one another. That after-baby schedule I made? It involved people I thought would help me. I wanted my husband to stay home and watch our son, which was challenging given that he was in language class for twenty hours a week and also leading our ministry team. I thought my friend Jenny could watch my son occasionally. It didn't occur to me that her three-month-old might take up all her spare moments. There was an expectation in my mind that I wouldn't have to go it alone. A healthy desire to be sure, but really, my expectations for others were unrealistic. As much as they wanted to help me, they could not meet all my needs.

I had expectations on my son, too. I expected him to be cool with the schedule I prescribed. (And actually, he was pretty cool with it. I think that was God saying, "This girl needs to be *eased* into parenting.") I assumed we would bond well and it never crossed my mind that he might not want to breastfeed, take naps, or poop on time with the schedule.

I grew up with a mom who loves hosting; it seemed her particular delight if I brought home a crowd of friends unexpectedly. Within minutes there would be drinks and snacks spanning the counter. That was her element. But my mother-in-law, probably like most people, appreciates a little warning for extra guests. She too is a gracious hostess, but prefers some time to prepare, and a level of decorum which is often lost in my home. It took us years to realize that we had different expectations on one another. I thought she didn't really want me to come over and she thought I was rather presumptuous in my casual approach to her home. We both came into our relationship with expectations.

It wasn't until I began to take Ethan outside for walks that I realized I had an expectation that people would trust my judgment as a parent. They did not. We had moved to a culture where it takes a village to raise a child, and that includes telling the new mama exactly what she is doing wrong.

In new seasons, we can easily and unknowingly put an unrealistic weight on the people around us to be and do what we need. And when expectations don't meet reality, disappointment follows. While there will be people who want to help us, our unchecked expectations don't make space for others to offer us what they can actually give.

EXPECTATIONS IN SCRIPTURE

To see a clear example of expectations in Scripture, we can look back again to the Israelites.

For generations, the Israelites were slaves in Egypt but finally their day of deliverance arrives. They escape Pharaoh by way of the Red Sea, and Moses and his sister rejoice with a song about it. They seem pretty content in their newfound freedom for a few days until they realize they have been led into a place without water.

I can't be too harsh on the Israelites. Water is a basic human need and access to it is not an unreasonable expectation. Transitions have a way of bringing us down to ground zero. And according to Maslow's hierarchy of needs, the physiological needs come first. So Moses threw a piece of wood into the water and made it sweet, and the people were mollified. For a while.

Until again, they came to a place where their needs were unmet. Grumbling, they said to Moses, "If only we had died by the LORD's hand in Egypt! There we sat around pots of meat and ate all the food we wanted, but you have brought us out into this desert to starve this entire assembly to death" (Exodus 16:3).

Again, the desire for food and water is normal and healthy. But I cannot say they embraced this change. They complained. They looked back with the belief that what they left behind was better. Think about that—they longed for slavery! But that only hardened their hearts to the situation they were in. They let the pain of their unmet expectations overwhelm their hearts and they lost sight of what God was doing in and for them.

I see myself in them. I don't always respond to unmet expectations with contentment and hope. My heart does not jump to, "I'll be okay. My needs will be met soon. God is still at work!" No, it is tempting to respond like the Israelites—to look back longingly at a previous situation and believe that it was better, or fall into despair that the present circumstances will never be what I want them to be.

We tend to forget the hard parts of a previous situation and romanticize it. Instead, we need to be honest about our former lives. Were they perfect? No. Were there things we didn't like? Yes. Most importantly, we need to recognize our expectations and navigate them with God's perspective instead of our own.

EXPECTATIONS AND GRACE

How do we enter into this mess of expectations? Some of us just try harder to make it work. We burn so much energy trying to be the gods of our own little worlds, making the pieces fit together, restless until we can feel like life matches our ideals. Idealism will push us into madness, striving to attain that which is just out of reach. Conversely, some of us convince ourselves that we don't need that much, that we can live with less, bringing the bar of our expectations down to meet reality.

One path leads to exhaustion and frustration, the other to bitterness and the shutting down of our hearts. God invites us to take another path—one of grace and hope.

Grace needs to show up in so many places in transition in order for us to embrace it fully. And it begins with giving grace to ourselves.

We need grace in the practical, daily moments to give ourselves permission to serve dinner on paper plates because we have no idea where the real ones are, to choose to take a deep breath and not beat ourselves up for not being able to find the new soccer field. With grace, we remind ourselves we are new at this. We let ourselves off the hook for not having it together, not being where we think we "should" be.

> Grace needs to show up in so many places in transition in order for us to embrace it fully. And it begins with giving grace to ourselves.

Most importantly, we give grace to the role expectations have in our lives. From my own experience, I've learned that there are three important principles to keep in mind with regard to expectations.

First, expectation fulfillment takes time. Most of our expectations involve gaining back some measure of what we have lost—friendships, some level of competence in the new culture, meaningful work to do. They are universal needs. It's natural that these will take time and it is likely that we will have them again, eventually. With these expectations, we have to just hang in there and be intentional about seeing them fulfilled. In the meantime, we live in grace and hope.

Second, we have to remember that our expectations may be met in different ways than we think. This is true particularly when the transition we have made is from one culture to another, even one city to another. Things operate differently. We have to examine how we think our expectations will be met. Grace helps loosen our grip on the means.

Third, there are some expectations that simply must die. Our children grew up in community where they rarely had friends who lived more than a minute or two away. In fact, during our last two years overseas, we knew around sixty homeschooled kids within about a two-mile radius of us. Needless to say, our kids were never bored. But in the States, that's just not reality. There may be a few neighborhood kids to play with and that is a blessing, but the kind of community we had overseas was rare and not replicable. It won't be that way again and so we have to let that expectation go gracefully.

Transition takes its toll on us emotionally, physically, and spiritually. I have found that during transition, my relational and emotional capacity is more limited. I have to keep reminding myself that I have been through a lot and that it makes sense to pull back from activity and just rest my soul from all it has been through.

To be honest, that's not what I want to do, but this is where I rest in His presence.

EXPECTATIONS AND HOPE

Expectations spring from hope—hope for the transition, the new season, the new place. Yet, we are often disappointed. Why?

Perhaps because we are hoping in the wrong things.

We hope for certain outcomes. We hope we will find a good church, a safe place to live, new friends. People feed into this when we move, by saying things like, "You'll make new friends. It'll just take time." So is that where I should plant my hope? Unintentionally, we encourage people in the wrong direction. We know people mean well, and in some sense they are right—most likely, I will find friends again. But that's not where my hope should be. Our hope is in the God who goes before us, who sees our needs and will care for us.

M. Craig Barnes in his book *When God Interrupts* says, "When we have focused too narrowly on the dream we thought the Savior would give us, then it is the dream that has become the Savior, not Him."[1] This is where we examine our expectations, where we ask ourselves if we've put all our hope in our expectations being met, if our happiness and contentment have become defined by if-onlys. As good as they are, a good home, a church family, a new best friend are not what saves us. Instead, God calls us to remember that He alone saves. He is what we're really after.

Isaiah 49:23 says, "I am the LORD; those who hope in me will not be disappointed." Verse after verse encourages us to hope in the Lord. Yet, in practice, we add our own agenda: "I hope in the Lord, that He will give me. . . ." If we move into new seasons with a stranglehold on the way we expect life to go, we close our hearts to what God is doing. It sets us up for bitterness, disappointment, and frustration.

Instead, God asks us to loosen our grip on life, and in the process, our hearts will open to something new. He invites us to bring our expectations before Him with an attitude of hope, presenting our requests while trusting Him with the outcome. We put our hope not in the end result, but in God. He is the only One who will provide what we need, when we need it. Often, that's not the way or the timing we want. We are impatient, needy people. But He's also the One who gives us the grace to live in a place of need as we wait to see how He's working in our lives.

A few years after our move back to the States, the last dredges of unmet expectations from this move were still acutely hanging over us as a family. We still longed for the kids to have solid friendships in the neighborhood, our son to find his niche, and I still wanted to figure out my ministry role. I spent so much energy trying to meet these expectations on my own. I was constantly making suggestions to the kids, trying to nudge them this way or that. I kept strategizing options; there was a scheming quality to my life.

> He invites us to bring our expectations before Him with an attitude of hope, presenting our requests while trusting Him with the outcome.

One day, I sensed God telling me, "You know, Gina, all those things you are trying to make happen—I can make them happen. But you have to trust me to do it in my time and my ways. And there might be things on that list that I don't think need to happen. You need to trust me with that too."

So I gave up. I let go, mostly because I was tired and that's a good impetus for letting someone else take control. I wrote a list of all the expectations I had for life here. And at the top, I penned, "If they need to happen, He'll make them happen."

For months, I pulled out that list each morning. I didn't pray through them because I found that when I did, I started to scheme again. I simply held the list out and prayed, "God, I'm hoping in you for this."

You know what? Those expectations began to be met. It was like watching a garden grow. First, the glimpses of green peeking through the dirt, promises of future life. Each bud spoke God's presence to me: "I see you. I see what you need. I'm providing for you, far better than you can do for yourself. Trust me. Give it time."

We are often unaware of the mental energy we spend on trying to manipulate our world into the shape we desire. Inevitably, that leads to anxiety, frustration, and disappointment. It leads us away from God. Instead, He calls us to come to Him. I found it so helpful to name my expectations, to lay those hopes at His feet, and then step away.

I said at the beginning of this chapter that desire and expectations go hand in hand. To make peace with change, we realize our expectations and lay them at His feet. But to bring our expectations to God is to let them go. It means to surrender control over how and when they will be met. In the end, expectation management involves trusting that He sees our needs and cares enough to meet them in His ways and in His timing.

And, see, there's the rub. I do not like this timeline of His. Yet, this is when we learn what it means to be at peace while we wait.

CHAPTER EIGHT

Staying Anchored

I WAS OUT RUNNING ONE NIGHT WHEN I PULLED a hip muscle. I was frustrated that I had to put a pause on running, but I figured it would only be for a short time. I gave it several weeks, but the minute I ran again, the pain returned. I decided to give it a little more time. And again, when I tried running, it hurt. I asked a doctor to give me a cortisone shot for a quick fix. It lasted a few months and then the pain returned.

Nearly six months later, I went to a chiropractor. There, I learned that I pulled a muscle because years of exercising with poor form and minimal stretching had misaligned my hips. I was an injury waiting to happen.

It took nearly two years of chiropractic care to get my body straightened out. Through the process, I had a lot of work to do. I had to practice strengthening some parts of my body and stretching others. The night of my injury, I had no idea how long the road to recovery would be.

Sometimes, we bounce right back from transition. The challenges pass and we quickly recover our losses. God satisfies our desires and we find life to be what we hoped. But other times, the road back to solid ground is a longer journey than we imagine.

Sometimes we feel stuck in a holding pattern, like a plane circling the runway, waiting to land. Maybe it's two years in and you're still lonely. That job didn't pan out the way you hoped. We don't learn to be parents overnight. The adoption process stalls. You just can't find your niche. It's like trying to put a puzzle together but we're missing pieces.

Though we know God will provide, we still want certain things to happen. We want to feel competent right now. We want new friends yesterday. We don't want a learning curve. We want a short-cut to normal. We don't want to have to be sidelined. We want a cortisone shot to take away the pain.

The waiting is a raw and exposed place. Here we walk through challenges that don't dissipate overnight. We ache for what we've lost and we feel all our desire and unmet expectations. This is the in-between place where we do the hard work of learning to accept His assignments, trust in His character, and rest in His strength.

> It's in the waiting that we find that what we want most of all is not the gifts but the Giver.

While we might be willing to linger a little in the lessons, what do we do when He seems to take His sweet time rearranging our lives? It's one thing to drop anchor in the truth. It's another to doggedly hold on to it while the waves are pounding against us, threatening to pull us away from Him.

This in-between place is holy ground, where we learn to practice living deeply anchored in Him. This is the place where God calls us to seek His face, and where He invites us to trust and hope in Him on an intimate level. It's in the waiting that we find that what we want most of all is not the gifts but the Giver. We learn to be satisfied in Him alone.

This time is not wasted; it is where God helps us grow. That hip injury revealed a greater issue in my body that needed addressing, and sometimes transition is the setback we need to reset our souls.

STAYING ANCHORED IN SCRIPTURE

Let's revisit the story of the Israelites. It's easy to forget that after the flight from Egypt, their journey to the promised land took *forty years*. Imagine leaving slavery with the hope that you will finally receive God's promise, except it doesn't happen today. Or tomorrow. Or maybe even in your lifetime. But His timing is not our timing.

While we're fixed on the fulfillment of our needs, desires, and expectations, He's focused on our character. While we want a normal, productive life again as quickly as possible, He has plans to grow us. We want our comfort and happiness; He wants so much more for us. He is not slow in keeping His promises, yet our idea of slow is so very different.

The Israelites had to learn to keep coming back to the Lord in the desert. They had to become people who sought God, trusted in Him, and hoped in Him while they waited for the promised land.

God calls us to seek Him in these times of waiting; that is our first task. And as we seek, we do it with an attitude of expectancy. We hold fast with confidence that we will meet God wherever we are. As David says in Psalm 27, "My heart says of you, 'Seek his face!' Your face, LORD, I will seek. . . . I remain confident of this: I will see the goodness of the LORD in the land of the living. Wait for the LORD; be strong and take heart and wait for the LORD" (vv. 8, 13–14).

The word *wait* in the Old Testament is the Hebrew word *qavah*, which can also be translated *hope*. Hoping in God invites us to trust that though this new season may look different, it is still good. It means trusting that God knows what you need going in and that He will provide.

Proverbs 3:5–6 gives us a beautiful promise: "Trust in the LORD with all your heart, and do not lean on your own understanding. In all your ways acknowledge him, and he will make straight your paths" (ESV). Those unknown paths we find ourselves walking during transition are known to Him. We might not understand where they are taking us, but we don't need to. We need to trust.

Trusting is easier said than done. We hesitate to trust our hearts completely to God because it means stepping away from our own understanding of how life should work. It means letting go of what is known to embrace what we cannot see. And rather than continuing to force our situations into the shape of our choosing, trust calls us to wait on Him to work out the details of our lives.

Paula Reinhart writes, "Trust is living between longing and demand. It is a surrender to the particular means of trying to make our agendas happen. . . . Trust lies in the willingness to accept the particulars of how and when and where God chooses to intervene . . . . Trusting God is grounded in staking the whole of my being on the reality that He loves me." [1]

The good news is that God does not leave us to wait alone. He gives us the patience, grace, and strength to wait well. "Meanwhile, the moment we get tired in the waiting, God's Spirit is right alongside helping us along. If we don't know how or what to pray, it doesn't matter. He does our praying in and for us, making prayer out of our wordless sighs, our aching groans. He knows us far better than we know ourselves, knows our pregnant condition, and keeps us present before God. That's why we can be so sure that every detail in our lives of love for God is worked into something good" (Romans 8:26–28 MSG).

We will get tired in the waiting, but God is right there with us in it. He knows the intimate details of our lives and we can remain confident that we will see His favor. When we find ourselves in a place of waiting, let's actively seek God with hope and trust.

Staying Anchored by Seeking God

We had been told that we would live in Singapore for about two years. Once we had made the move, I found I was reluctant to embrace our new life. Without realizing it, I had hedged myself in. I didn't want to put down roots. I wanted my heart to stay safely closed.

Our friend, Ken, observed my reticence with sympathy. He had responded the same way when his family first moved there. After a time, he realized it wasn't helping his heart. He gave me this advice, "Take stock of your losses and your gains, and then focus on your gains."

Until now, so much of this book has focused on acknowledging our losses, which is important. But equally important is focusing on our gains.

After that conversation with my coworker, I decided that even though Singapore was not exactly what I thought I wanted, I would play the cards I'd been dealt. As it turned out, they were good cards.

The five years we spent in Singapore were some of the most transformational of my life.

> I believe God is in this new place to which He has brought me. I will actively seek out and affirm the ways He is at work.

In chapter 2, we talked about recognizing that God is good. Staying anchored means to continually seek evidence and acknowledge His goodness. And we begin by embracing a mindset that says, "I believe God is in this new place to which He has brought me. I will actively seek out and affirm the ways He is at work."

We Stay Anchored through Worship

In her book *The God Who Sees You*, Tammy Maltby tells about a time in her life when she and her husband waited on God to provide. They prayed together and afterwards she asked him, "What do we do now?"

Her husband answered, "We worship while we wait."

This is the posture we are all invited to. As Maltby says, it is "the choice that can keep us going day after day when the fog surrounds us and we can't see our hands in front of our faces."[2]

When we focus on our gains, we cannot help but see reasons to worship God. When we worship, we acknowledge the true worth of something. And when we worship God, we turn our eyes away from the world, away from our circumstances, and onto who He is.

Worship is not simply the obedient response to witnessing God at work in our lives. It does something necessary in our souls. It anchors us in all the ways we've talked about so far: it calls us to rejoice in His goodness, fixes our eyes on His character, and brings us back into a right position of dependence and trust in Him to provide. Worship enables us to celebrate that He is God even in the midst of our deepest sorrow.

The authors of *Hope for the Weary Mom* write, "See, the thing about worship is that it acknowledges in the very deepest part of our souls that we need him. We can't take this journey on our own. We aren't supposed to. Needing him every hour is not defeat. It is an appetite put there by God that only He can fill. Our daily moving toward him through worship is an acknowledgment that we were made for nothing less. We need the very presence of the Lord to strengthen and guide us. We need him every hour. Here is where we find hope."[3]

The more we worship, the more our hope grows. The more we look at Him, the more we trust Him. And the more we trust Him, the more content we are in times of waiting.

Some days are harder than others though. Some days the challenges overshadow what we know to be true about God, and worship feels false. How then, do we do it?

After a few years in the States, the life I had was still not the one I would have chosen in some ways. I was busier than I was in my previous seasons, stretched in more directions, and lonelier. I continued to wait on God for many things.

Sometimes, I grew frustrated and I wondered what good could come from waiting if I couldn't see any results. And then I turned to Habakkuk 3:17–18 and the picture it gives of walking through challenges with God at our side, our closest companion. It reads, "Though the fig tree should not blossom, nor fruit be on the vines, the produce of the olive fail and the fields yield no food, the flock be cut off from the fold and there be no herd in the stalls, yet I will rejoice in the LORD; I will take joy in the God of my salvation" (ESV).

This we call to mind, and this is where we plant our hope: Every day, God is with us. He faithfully walks with us, even in the waiting. He loves us too much to leave us in limbo. He's not done showing us His mercy. And as we wait, we draw as close to Him as we can get. The closer we get, the more inclined we are to worship.

In my own in-between place, it helped to write in my own circumstances into those verses. Something like this: "Though I'm still figuring this all out, and some days I have no one to talk to about it, though I still long for the past and I haven't found normal, yet I will rejoice in the Lord, I will take joy in the God of my salvation."

When the weight of our unmet expectations hangs heavy, this is a good place to begin. We name those places where we are still waiting, and we say, "yet. . . ."

Yet I will hope. Yet I will turn my eyes to God. Yet I will believe that He is everything He says He is. Yet I will trust in the Giver. Yet I will worship.

There is always a "yet" with God.

We Stay Anchored through Gratitude

Gratitude is the companion to worship. We turn our eyes to the Giver with worship, and we acknowledge His gifts to us, His favor on us, with gratitude. We may not see what we hope to see God doing, but we don't want to miss all that He *is* doing.

Living in America presents a complexity we didn't know in our thirteen years overseas. Overseas, our coworkers were also our friends, family, church fellowship, classmates, and "hanging out during kids' activities" people. One large social group. Nice and simple. God was faithful to provide consistent relationships throughout those years and by the time we left, there were many in that group with whom we'd been friends for over a decade.

Moving to America brought with it the complexity of having to juggle many different social groups. If our lives were a Venn diagram, there was almost no overlap between circles—our new school was far away from where we lived, our new soccer club was in another part of town, our church in another, and while our office was close by, most of our coworkers were not. Each new activity was in a different place and with a separate group of people, and the activities crowded our schedules to the point where I often wondered when and what we would eat. They involved medical release forms and coach fees and bringing cookies and all sorts of other little details.

It was tempting to look back and long for our simpler life, but I have become incredibly grateful for what we have here. I thank God that our kids can play soccer and archery and explore a new place and learn to call it home. I am thankful for new people in our lives who bless us and make me wonder how we lived without them before. Our life was simple in Asia in part because our options were limited and we had to learn to live without. I am grateful for abundance.

Gratitude can feel like panning for gold. Sometimes, we find big, shiny pieces just waiting for us to pick them up and turn them around in the light. These are the times when I see our kids light up with renewed life, or I hang up the phone after a good talk with a new friend. I shut my eyes and blink back the tears and say, "God, you are so good to us!"

But other times, practicing gratitude is more like sifting for specks of gold mixed in with the mud. We hunt for the truth, the glimmers of goodness.

We train our eyes to search for those little bits and rejoice in them because they are valuable, and they remind us that we are in the hands of the One who blesses. When we find them, we scoop them up and treasure them, and realize we are deeply blessed and incredibly rich.

We might not always experience the big nuggets of victory, but we can claim the gold dust of everyday grace—the breath in our lungs and feet that carry us and hands that work and eyes that see. It's salvation and grace and life and His love and presence and all that cannot be taken from us even in the darkest moments.

The more we pan for gold, the more we see it. We see gold in a kind word, a safe drive, a quiet moment. We see gold in sunrises and fresh air and the fresh beginning that comes with each new day.

We are not asked to give thanks for every circumstance, but *in* every circumstance. Whatever the season brings, there's gold to be found at your feet. We can practice gratitude even in the waiting. We can find evidence of goodness mixed with the dirt of hardship. We can search for the reminders that we are never forsaken, even when the road is rough.

When we thank Him for who He is and how we see Him at work in our lives, we shift our focus from what we still long to have to all that He is giving us.

Gratitude anchors us in God's presence. As Kristen Strong writes in *Girl Meets Change*, "Gratitude provides a window to a windowless room."[4]

When we thank Him for who He is and how we see Him at work in our lives, we shift our focus from what we still long to have to all that He is giving us.

We Are Satisfied in Him

In seeking to stay anchored, we must see that the losses, desires, and expectations that surface in transition all reveal something good and necessary in us—but they are not what we want. We want Him. Lamentations 3:24–25 confirms this: "I say to myself, 'The LORD is my portion; therefore, I will wait for him.' The LORD is good to those whose hope is in him, to the one who seeks him."

In *The Allure of Hope*, Jan Meyers writes, "God fences us in. He destroys the vineyards we create to satisfy ourselves. He then takes us to that dark place where the only way out is to be found. We discover that we cannot move, and in so doing we are surprised with how much we were meant to be still. We discover we have expended useless energy in coming up with our own provisions, and we are caught off guard with how *enough* He is." [5]

We were meant to be still. God leaves us in holding patterns to bring us to this reality: He is enough. We stop fighting when we rest in that truth. We stop scrambling, stop trying to feed ourselves on lesser things. In this place, we find peace. Like the Israelites, we trust Him to give us manna every morning.

Ultimately, what we want is Jesus. He is our manna.

In the midst of transition, it doesn't feel like we want Him the most. We want a friend, or a new church, or the boxes to be unpacked. We want to feel settled. But even when we have all those things, our souls will still hunger for more. In this desert place, we learn to seek Him above all else.

"God takes everyone he loves through a desert," writes Paul Miller. "It is his cure for our wandering hearts, restlessly searching for a new Eden. After awhile you notice your real thirst. The desert is God's best hope for the creation of an authentic self. The desert becomes a window to the heart of God. He finally gets your attention because He's the only game in town. The best gift in the desert is God's presence." [6]

When I look back on the transitions I have gone through, I am certainly thankful for the times when life corrected itself quickly. We have walked into new seasons that were far more abundant than what we had left behind. But there is a sweetness, too, in reflecting on the seasons when new life took time to grow. There, God met us. He stripped away other sources of life and taught us to drink deeply from Him alone. I have come to understand what Peter meant in John 6:67–68 when, in response to Jesus's question, "You do not want to leave too, do you?" He replied, "To whom shall we go? You have the words of eternal life."

Where else could any of us go to find life? So we stay anchored—we seek Him, rest in His presence, and trust that He is enough for us. And we hold onto the truth that He is working something good in us. As Tammy Maltby explains, "It's not just plodding, grit-your-teeth waiting. . . . Instead, it's moving along with your head up—moving in expectation, because you really expect that something's going to happen. Because you know that whether you can see it or not, the God of the universe is at work in your life and in the world. He will keep His promises. He will show up when the time is right—when His time is right." [7]

To stay anchored, we practice what we know. We hope in His goodness and trust in His sovereignty to shape our paths. We don't squirm away from our weakness but instead let it push us to Him. We loosen the grip we hold on our expectations and let go, then we cling to Him like our lives depend on it because they do. We worship. We thank Him for what we see and trust Him for what we don't. And we enjoy Him—our anchor, and our way home.

CHAPTER NINE

Navigating Grief

ABOUT THREE YEARS INTO OUR TIME IN SINGA-
pore, the string of goodbyes began in earnest. Many of the families
we had become friends with had come to the end of their terms
and were asked to move back to their home countries. One family
had two boys with whom our son had grown close. Their flight
left in the morning, and we decided to get up early and say a final
farewell to them at the airport.

As we hugged and cried and said our goodbyes, I noticed Ethan
hiding behind a pillar. I called him over. He shook his head. I walked
over and tried to reason with him, but he would have none of it.
In the end, I physically carried him over and pushed him toward
the arms of his friends. The second they hugged, the dam burst.

I felt horrible pushing my child into grief. But I knew the decision he made that day—to move toward or away from his pain—would set the course for how he responded to his heart in future sorrows. He needed to step toward it, for the sake of his own soul.

So much of what we have looked at—acknowledging hard places, identifying what we have lost, exposing our desires, examining expectations—raises areas of grief in our hearts. Grief is never fun to navigate. It is something we want to avoid at all costs, or at the very least, move through quickly. It feels counter to "be joyful always." But grief is a significant part of transition and we need to develop a practice of grieving well so that we stay wholehearted. How do we do that? It starts with seeing grief as a companion on the journey, rather than an enemy to be conquered.

GRIEF AS OUR COMPANION

One of my favorite books is *Hind's Feet on High Places*. In it, the main character, Much Afraid, is called to go to the High Places by the Good Shepherd. He gives her two companions: Sorrow and Suffering. She is baffled that the Good Shepherd would give her these two to guide her. I read that book in college and at that time, I cannot say I was acquainted with grief. I had the same response as Much Afraid to the prospect of having sorrow and suffering be any part of my journey.

Years later, I have come to see that sorrow and suffering do indeed come along for the journey. I am learning that they are, albeit unwelcome, good companions.

I am coming to know them better. That is what "acquainted" means, after all. Most of us dedicate a lot of effort to avoiding sorrow and suffering. As Christians, we tend to believe that if we experience them, we must somehow be lacking in faith. Me, I just want to avoid them because they are not pleasant.

In time, I've come to know grief as a gift. It helps us feel deeply and see how much our hearts have been opened to love. To deny it is not only to be untruthful about the impact a person, place, or situation has had on us, but it closes our hearts to the future. Denial of grief does not make the pain go away—it merely shames it and hides it away for another time.

The American culture has a narrow view of grief, though, which revolves mainly around grieving the death of a loved one. When someone dies, we give mourners time to grieve, although even here there seems to be a statute of limitations on how long grief is appropriate.

In truth, grief is much broader. We feel loss in large and small ways, in unexpected losses, in repeated loss. Our narrow view keeps us from seeing those losses and grieving them well. As a result, the grief expresses itself in other ways—anger, despondency, frustration, and confusion. These emotions are often a smoke screen, an outer layer that protects us from feeling deeper, more vulnerable emotions. If we push past them, we will find our grief.

Many of the emotional challenges we've talked about in earlier chapters result from not giving ourselves space to grieve. We need to grieve what we miss and who. We need to allow ourselves to mourn the loss of connection, competence, contribution, and ultimately, identity. We need to grieve the areas where life is not what we thought it would be.

> To deny it is not only to be untruthful about the impact a person, place, or situation has had on us, but it closes our hearts to the future.

We fool ourselves if we believe that we can ignore grief. Unprocessed emotion doesn't go away. It will continue to manifest itself in the outward emotions

I mentioned earlier. Or we become numb to other emotions, losing our capacity for joy as well as sorrow.

Rather than hiding or denying grief, what does it look like to walk side by side with sorrow on the journey through transitions?

GIVING OURSELVES PERMISSION TO GRIEVE

One of Pixar's most popular movies, *Inside Out*, shows us something about grief. It centers on Riley, a young girl whose family has moved from Minnesota to California. She struggles to stay her parents' "happy girl" as she misses friends and activities from back home. Inside her head, we see Joy and Sadness, two emotional personas, responding to Riley's experiences in a variety of ways to maintain equilibrium. Their goal, it seems, is to create as many happy memories as possible.

Sadness says things like, "We could cry until we can't breathe," and, "Crying helps me slow down and obsess over the weight of life's problems." She is a bit of a downer, to say the least. And Joy works intently to keep Sadness contained.

As the plot escalates and Riley begins to whirl through every emotion, Joy realizes that Riley really doesn't need to be restricted to just happy experiences. She needs to be free to feel the grief over what she has lost. In a pivotal moment, Joy gives Sadness Riley's most precious memories, and allows her to change them from happy to sad, which allows Riley to fully enter and process her new reality.[1]

When I watched this scene in the theater, someone in the audience muttered, "What is she *doing*?" But I cried tears of relief because it was exactly what needed to happen. When Joy gives Sadness the reins, Riley is able to express her pain and begin to embrace her new place.

We, too, need this permission to grieve. As fellow blogger J.R. Forasteros writes, "We are so afraid of sadness that we've shut ourselves off from the gift of grief. We've convinced ourselves that Joy is the opposite of Sadness, that we have to be happy all the time, that sadness makes us weak."[2]

One night during our move back to the States, we were talking as a family about how we were doing. (Our children grew to hate the question, "So how are you *feeling*?") As we talked, our son became emotional and said, "I don't want to talk about it. Whenever I start to think about it, I avoid it!"

We took a pause as a family to admit that yes, we'd all like to avoid thinking about it sometimes. Then we talked about how instead, it might be better to give ourselves moments when we do let ourselves think about it, to let ourselves feel the depth of our loss and weep over it. We don't need to cry constantly through the transition process, but we do need to honor our hearts and our emotions. This is the freedom we need to give ourselves to feel what is true. And it might be the hardest part of transition to own.

GRIEF IN SCRIPTURE

Throughout Scripture we read stories of people willing to grieve, people like Hannah in 1 Samuel or the writer of Lamentations. We have already looked at Job, grieving the horrific losses of his family and livelihood. King David wrote seventy-six of the 150 Psalms and the majority centered on themes of lament.

And then I think of Jesus, the "man of sorrows . . . acquainted with grief" (Isaiah 53:3 ESV). Of all the things we could have been told about Him, we know this detail. I don't doubt that Jesus was a man who exuded joy, who could throw His head back and laugh. But we are told specifically that He was no stranger to sorrow and grief. Why? I think to tell us, "It's okay. This is part of the journey." If Jesus chose to walk with sorrow and suffering, it is to be our path as well.

In *A Sacred Sorrow*, Michael Card tells us, "At every major turning point of His ministry, Jesus pours out His heart in lament—when He enters Jerusalem for the last time, when He experiences His final meal with the disciples, when He struggles with the Father in the Garden of Gethsemane, and most importantly, when He endures the suffering of the cross. Jesus understood the honesty represented in the life that knows how to lament."[3]

If Jesus knew grief, He knows what it is like for us. Through recent transitions, God has encouraged me to take the hands of Sorrow and Suffering. I confess, it still throws me when I encounter grief in the presence of others because I'm still not particularly comfortable with expressing sorrow unexpectedly and publicly. But I am learning to be grateful because I sense it means my heart is being opened by grief, that it is developing in me a greater capacity to enter into the heartache of others and to say, "I am coming to know this too."

WAVES OF GRIEF

It would be wonderful if grief were linear. We would all appreciate a definite ending point—"After one year, I will be done grieving." The truth is, grief is unpredictable. It comes and goes, and surprises us in unexpected moments.

When we left Singapore and returned to the closed country we'd lived in previously, we were reunited with our good friends, Dan and Jenny, and their family. We thought it would last forever, or at least a good long time. It was only a few months into our reunion that they took us out to dinner and told us that they had only one more year overseas.

What resulted was something my husband and I called "The Great Sadness." It was something of a cloud that hung over us the whole year. Most of the time it was small and not too bothersome, a little like a little cloud hovering overhead. Other times the cloud would break and shower down the reality of the inevitable. Like the day I was driving a group of the neighbor kids home from kung fu class. Our daughter and her two best friends, who didn't know that they would be heading in three different directions the next summer talked in the back seat about how they would *always* be best friends and live together. I swallowed a lump in my throat and thought, "Now God? Seriously? I'm driving! I can't handle this right now!"

I managed to get home, close the door to my bedroom, and have a good cry. I never knew when those moments of grief would come upon me.

Recently, a friend I knew overseas also made the move back to the States and settled into our city. She called me one night, over-whelmed by the stress of transition. The cell reception in her home was so terrible we were cut off. I called her back immediately but it took several rings for her to answer. When she finally did, she was in tears. That moment caught her in the simple grief of not being able to have a conversation when she needed it. I get that.

Grief caught me off guard a few days after our move back to the States, when a news story about our former city came on television and I felt the tears flow down my cheeks. It blew over me when I met up with old friends one summer and enjoyed long conversations that made me ache for a place here where I felt that comfortable more often. It touched me when I heard other languages spoken and I remembered that I am no longer an expat. It whispered to me when I saw my friend in a job she loves while I was still looking for my niche.

I hadn't planned on grieving in any of those moments, but they happened. This is the way of grief: we can't predict what or when it will be triggered, but I hope we can give it space.

After this most recent transition, I kept imagining myself as someone wading in the ocean, slowly walking toward shore. At first, the waves of grief had the potential to knock me over. The closer I have come to shore, the smaller the waves tended to be, but still they came at unexpected times and with unexpected intensity. Just when I thought I'd found my footing, another wave would come sneaking up and shove me off balance.

The waves will keep coming for a time. It does not mean we are not doing well—it means we are in process. The more we move toward the solid ground God provides, the more we will be able to navigate the waves of grief.

Managing Grief

I've heard people describe themselves as pre-grievers and post-grievers—people who tend to express their grief about a loss beforehand, and on the other side are ready to move on quickly, or seem to be unaffected by the loss until it is past, and then the grief hits them.

I wonder about the truth of this. In the months leading up to or following a big life change, I have found that there are mixed emotions. We might be excited about the next chapter, but we dread leaving the one we are in. We anticipate the change, but at the same time we do not want it to come. It is heart-wrenching at times to hold these conflicting emotions all at once.

When we say we are pre-grievers or post-grievers, I wonder if we are simply finding a way to cope with this tension.

Some transitions are harder than others, and there may be more to look forward to in certain cases than others, which makes it easier to move on. But in the process of being wholehearted, it is important to be honest with ourselves about whether we are giving grief freedom to be.

When our good friends were preparing to move to other countries and we were planning to move closer to the office, I vacillated between excitement about our new apartment and the accompanying proximity to coworkers, and the devastation of our friends leaving. When I started to focus on being excited about our move, I felt like I was betraying our friends. On the other hand, when I let myself feel the grief of the loss, I felt ungrateful for all that God had provided for us. Holding these two valid yet conflicting emotions at the same time felt like my heart might explode. It is easier just to feel one or the other.

Whether we are inclined to pre-grieve or post-grieve, it is good to recognize our tendency in these responses. Do I call myself a post-griever because I do not want to engage with how I am feeling now about the impending loss? Am I calling myself a pre-griever because I am just done with pain and want to get over it? Reflective people might tend to lean toward pre-grieving, while others may not realize the full impact of a transition until after the fact. Ultimately, we are doing our best to minimize the pain. But minimizing pain will minimize our joy.

Either way, we need to recognize that there is another option. The key is to anchor ourselves in the present. Physically, spiritually, emotionally, we need to live fully in the pain and the joy of today. This is the tension in which we live. To be where we are, in the present, is the wholehearted choice.

Our family learned this through a revolving door of expat relationships during our time overseas. After a couple years in Singapore, I introduced our then five-year-old son to a new kid at church. Ethan's first question to me was, "Well, how long is he going to be here?" Already, he was hedging bets in his heart about where he would invest emotionally, and it broke my heart. He was determined to avoid grief, but in the process, he missed out on a friendship.

Our last year overseas, a new couple, Clint and Sung, moved to our city to join our work team. We connected immediately. In fact, within a week, they had already eaten dinner at our house several times and claimed the extra seats in our car for rides around town. The problem? Erik and I knew we were moving back to the States the next summer.

To be where we are, in the present, is the wholehearted choice.

I wanted to warn Sung that I was a bad investment—better to put her energy into someone who was going to stick around longer. I mentioned this thought to our mutual friend Katie and she said, "Don't! Just be friends with her."

So I was. Three months later, I broke the sad news to Sung. We cried, and agreed that it was good I didn't tell her earlier. Was it hard to say goodbye? Brutal. Was I glad I'd pursued her anyway? She remains a dear friend to this day.

In the movie *Shadowlands*, C. S. Lewis asks his wife, Joy, why we go through goodbyes when they are so painful. She replies, "The pain then is part of the joy now." [4] If it isn't hard to say goodbye, then maybe these places and these people have not meant that much to you. But if they have, rejoice. Celebrate. The sadness now means that it has been good, that it's been a gift.

DOING WELL IS GRIEVING WELL

When Erik and I move to a new place, we unpack and settle in like we are gunning for a new HGTV show, *Instant House*. When people share that they still have boxes unpacked after years of living somewhere, I am baffled. Do you not need that stuff? Usually within a week of moving, we're 90 percent unpacked. That's just how we roll.

And when people visit, they take a look around and say, "Wow, you're doing so well!"

It is a phrase people throw around a lot, "doing well." It feels like the finish line we are all racing toward in transition. I want to be the one to get there first. I'll run across, triumphant, hang my gold medal around my neck, and others can look at me and say, "Wow, look at her. She's doing *so well*."

But maybe an instant house or a jump back into productivity are not what denotes "doing well" in transition.

When it comes to grief, the unspoken assumption is that we are doing well when we don't look like we are grieving. We smile and continue to function and respond graciously with comments like, "God's blessing us!" and "It's hard but *good*." (We love that phrase too, don't we?)

But what if doing well in transition is being messy? What if it means the boxes stay unpacked for a while because instead we're doing soul work? What if it's needing to stop regularly just to have a good cry? What if it means we do less but feel more? What if it looks like us not being ourselves because we've lost part of who we were and we're willing to grieve the loss before we scramble back to creating identity?

There is a fear many of us hold that if we move into grief, we might never come out. We worry that we will become self-pitying, depressed shadows of our former selves. I'm not saying there is no danger of this. There is an art to walking into dark places and wrestling with what we find there, all the while anchoring ourselves to the truth and to God as our lifeline. It's a messy process, because we are messy people. But my hope in the end is that we are more and more redeemed people, people who bravely walk with God through every corner of our hearts and come out more open, more confident, and more grounded in Him.

To quote J. R. Forasteros again, "In choosing to grieve, we learn to worship the God who grieves with us. We learn the gift of saying 'Me too.' We learn the gift of grief, that sadness leads to joy, that Sunday always follows Friday, that death does not have the final word."[5]

Grief is here with us. And we need to take it by the hand and walk. If we do, we will find greater peace in the midst of change.

"Poet Max Dunaway, in the summer of 1970, told a young woman, 'If you think your heart is going to break, rather let it overflow.' Max explained that the assumed outcome is that losses break the heart. However, grieving well means the loss will be carried, held, embraced, incorporated, evidenced, remembered, and cherished like a fine aged wine after the plump ripened grape has long been distilled. During grief, the heart can pour out love and be relieved, not broken. Grief is held like the screaming newborn: it nurses, calms down, grows up, and moves out to nourish others."[6]

We are not meant to stop at simply acknowledging the sorrow in our hearts, but to find a new place to live from. In transition, God shakes us loose from old familiar places of the heart so that we can start this new chapter more firmly grounded in Him, and more deeply connected with others.

CHAPTER TEN

Anchored Together

RETURNING TO THE STATES WAS THE HARDEST transition I have ever experienced. I tried to navigate it by remembering all I had learned before—staying awake in my heart to what I was feeling, acknowledging the weight of all that changed for me and my family, sitting with my desires and honoring them as valid. Despite that, or maybe because of all that, I was a mess for months.

Thankfully, I was invited to join a small group of women discussing *I Thought It Was Just Me (but it isn't)* by Brené Brown, a book on recognizing shame and building shame resilience. We called it our "shame group," which sounds terrible but we went with it.

Most of these women had lived overseas and understood what I was going through. In them I found a safe place where I could share the challenges I was struggling with. I could bring my loss, desire, expectations, and honesty to them. Yet, it wasn't easy. Every week, I went to my group thinking, "Okay, pull it together, Gina. You're doing well today. This is the week you are *not* going to cry in front of these women." And every week, I cried.

But I also found healing. I moved closer to making peace with change through the space they gave me to grieve, and the validation they gave to my experience. I honestly don't know how I would have navigated that season without them. They were the lifesaver God tossed to me in deep waters.

Journeying with others can be one of the most healing aspects of moving into a new season of life. We need people to help carry our burdens, show us the ropes, offer shoulders to cry on, and to form our new normal with. Unfortunately, connecting can require the greatest amount of time and energy from us in a place where we are so often running on empty.

People who walked with me in the mess of transition have become some of the greatest means of grace God has given me. There are some who have walked with me every step of the way, others come for a season, others just for a moment. These women gave me grace, and they also encouraged me to give grace to myself.

Finding people who will help anchor our hearts in God is essential, but journeying with others involves a level of risk. Not everyone will welcome our mess. And when our paths join the paths of others, comparison often shows up too. Hopefully, though, in the process of inviting others to journey with us, we will become the kind of travel companion others need. After all, we were created to do this life together.

The Call to Walk with Each Other in Scripture

Recently, I spoke at a retreat about the fact that our souls need others. God crafted us in that way. A review of the phrase "each other" in Scripture reveals the myriad of ways we were created to interact: we are called to love, encourage, forgive, build up, pray for, be devoted to, live in harmony with, accept, instruct, serve, bear with, admonish, offer hospitality to, and belong to each other.

One of the most beautiful pictures of this kind of belonging is found in the book of Ruth. After Naomi's husband and two sons died, she found herself in an unwanted season. She determined to return to her homeland in Judah, to go back to what she knew. She encouraged her two daughters-in-law to stay behind in their own country. While one daughter-in-law, Orpah, did stay, Ruth insisted on going with Naomi. She told Naomi, "Do not urge me to leave you or to return from following you. For where you go I will go, and where you lodge I will lodge. Your people shall be my people, and your God my God" (Ruth 1:16 ESV).

Ruth committed to walking through transition with Naomi, and to doing it in the context of God's grace. We are called to walk together not just in transition, but in the Christian life. We are called to belong to each other, most of all in challenging times.

Galatians 6:2 charges us to "Carry each other's burdens, and in this way you will fulfill the law of Christ." To carry each other's burdens is to fulfill the call to love one another. As fellow travelers,

I will carry you through this transition and you can carry me the next time around.

But to carry each other's burdens requires us to admit them. It means we have to invite others into the hard things. We need to be honest about what we have lost, where we feel weak, how we are grieving. We have to set aside the guilt and shame that our enemy heaps on us for needing others. We have to remember the truth that needing others is the way our souls were made. It is an opportunity to be blessed and to be a blessing. Like Ruth and Naomi, we journey through transition with our eyes open, looking for travel companions.

FINDING THE GRACE GIVERS

A few months into our time back in the States, I chatted with an older gentleman about our move. When I told him about our son, he asked with a grin, "You got that kid Americanized yet?"

It was a joking comment, but it reminded me that so many people don't understand what certain transitions are like. Ethan, for whom America was a new, foreign country, was not Americanized yet. He probably will never feel fully American. I was tempted to be angry, but I chose to shake it off and move on.

Weeks later, I joined a party at the house of a friend from overseas. Among the partygoers were a number of people who had also spent time living in other countries. The conversations that night were peppered with comments like, "So this one time in Thailand . . ." and, "When I was flying to . . ."

These are my people, I thought.

We all need to find our people. Our people are the ones who get it. Who've been there. Whether it's the experience of living cross-culturally, having been through a similar stage of life, or just knowing what it's like to be the new kid on the block, we need to find the people who understand.

We will meet people who don't know what we're going through, and will struggle to give us permission to not be okay. They won't understand why we can't just get over it. But we don't have to take that to heart. We smile, and nod, and then keep searching for the grace givers—the ones who give us the time and space to navigate the road God has led us to. Because those are also the people who will help anchor us back to God.

In the process of making peace with change, our enemy will do his best to stop us. He desperately wants us to *not* be wholehearted, God-dependent people. He wants us to do transition in isolation, to feed us lies that we are lacking, failing, not enough, and misunderstood.

That's not what God has for us. God sends us people in transition to walk with us, to be rocks we can rest on, to guide us back to Him on the days when it's just too hard. They offer us compassion, grace, a listening ear, an empathetic word. They can speak truth to us when we have forgotten it. They lend us strength to stay in the process as long as it takes for God to do His work of grounding our souls in Him.

There was that day when I had to drive Ethan and his friend, Jackson, to their end-of-the-year middle-school party. I was coming off a few weeks of transition turmoil and I didn't think I had it in me to socialize with middle-school moms I had barely begun to know (and who, due to their small school, had known each other for years). I just couldn't muster the emotional energy to move toward them. But Jackson's mom, Jenny, called a mom at the party and asked her to make sure I felt included. Thus, I survived.

At first, we might only find a person here or there. We won't know everyone on the soccer team, but a lifeline phone call will get you through. We may not make connections with all the moms but just the one who takes the time to welcome you in.

When I was a new mom, that person for me was my friend Jenny. Her son was only three months older than mine but in my newbie mind that made her the expert. After an awful day nursing, I called Jenny and asked her to come give me advice. She didn't know what to tell me, but to be honest, I didn't care. I just needed someone to be with me in that moment and say, "I get it." She sat and talked with me while I muddled through. That was enough.

> Whatever season God has brought us into, no matter how hard it is or what shame it raises, someone else knows what it feels like.

My friend Ali reflected on how her transition into motherhood was a fairly smooth one simply because she did it in community. She had several friends who were a step ahead of her on the journey. They normalized the struggles she encountered and responded to her with grace and empathy. Those women were her grace givers.

Sometimes it's a challenge to find the people, or even one person, who truly understands. And sometimes, what God reveals in our hearts in transition is deeper and more challenging than what others can carry well for us. In these times, the grace you need may be found in professional help. While I have pursued community in each transition, I have also recognized times when the issues God was showing me required the wisdom and advice of a counselor. So I saw a counselor. There is no shame in this—it's an act of both humility and courage. It's a way to fight for the grace we need in the mess.

If you find yourself stuck in the same thought patterns, stuck in grief, stuck in some aspect of processing, it may be the time to ask a counselor, therapist, or other professional to be your grace giver. Doing so opens us up to receiving another means of God's redemptive love.

Through the years, I've learned that whatever season God has brought us into, no matter how hard it is or what shame it raises, someone else knows what it feels like. Someone else is walking through it, or has been there too. We are not alone. Our situation is not so unique that no one else can empathize. In the same way that our interests draw us to other people and help us connect, our pain connects us with others. Transitions are meant to be shared and mutually carried.

Yet to find our people, we have to be vulnerable.

BEING VULNERABLE TOGETHER

Few things make us as vulnerable as transitions. Our hearts get cracked open, our longings raw and exposed. Finding those who will handle our fragility is tricky, but worth the risk.

The word *vulnerable* comes from the Latin word *vulnerare*, which means "to be wounded." When we choose to be vulnerable with others, we are showing them our weakest places—the places that, if rejected, would cause us the greatest pain.

Why would we do that? Why did I keep going back to the book discussion group where I was sure the women thought I was emotionally unstable? I went because they accepted my mess. Not only that, but it seemed to draw them to me. My openness gave them permission to be open as well. This is the power of vulnerability and why it is a gift to us in transition.*

Brené Brown writes:

> We can't opt out of the uncertainty, exposure, and emotional risks that are woven through our daily experiences. Like it or not, vulnerability is coming, and we have to decide if we're going to open up to it or push it away.
>
> The only choice we really have is how we're going to respond to feeling vulnerable. And contrary to popular belief, our shields don't protect us. They simply keep us from being seen, heard, and known. . . . Our willingness to own and engage with our vulnerability determines the depth of our courage and the clarity of our purpose.
>
> Even if letting ourselves be seen and opening ourselves up to judgment or disappointment feels terrifying, the alternatives are worse: Choosing to feel nothing—numbing. Choosing to perfect, perform, and please our way out of vulnerability. Choosing rage, cruelty or criticism. Choosing shame and blame. Like most of you reading this, I have some experience with all of these alternatives, and they all lead to the same thing: disengagement and disconnection. [1]

Vulnerability is not optional if we want others to walk with us in transition.

My friend Ali, who I mentioned earlier, came to a place about six months into motherhood when she felt like she couldn't continue to fulfill her work responsibilities on top of being a new mom. She shared the struggle with her friend Lori, who listened well and gave her permission to express all she was feeling. It was the first time Ali had been vulnerable with Lori and it became a turning point in their relationship, taking their friendship to a deeper level.

When we open ourselves to others, we become the safe places for one another God wants us to be. Vulnerability is the path to remaining openhearted as we navigate transition.

"Sensitivity is a sign of life," writes Jeff Brown. "Better hurt than hardened. I bow to those who keep their hearts open when it is most difficult, those who refuse to keep their armor on any longer than they have to, those who recognize the courage at the

> **Vulnerability is the path to remaining openhearted as we navigate transition.**

heart of vulnerability. After all the malevolent warriors end each other, the open-hearted will inherit the earth." [2]

The openhearted and vulnerable walk courageously in defiance of the enemy. Yet, there is another tactic Satan will employ. If he cannot keep us from drawing close to others, he will use our proximity to cause us to compare our journeys with theirs.

THE COMPARISON TRAP

One of the greatest obstacles in embracing any assignment God has for us is comparison. When we're in a new chapter in life, the temptation to compare only grows. We long for some standard, some measuring stick that tells us we're making it, that we're doing okay. The old rules about how life usually works have changed on us, and we are searching for something that says, "Here's how you do this new chapter."

Instead of looking to Him for how to live it, we look to others who are seemingly in the same situation. If we're new moms, we look to other parents. If we're in a new city, we look to neighbors. When we begin to do that, comparison becomes the whisper in our ears, telling us where we come up short.

As a new mom, I looked at other moms in our ministry. Seemingly, we were all in the same boat. And in many ways, we were. In other ways though, we were completely different. We were wired differently. We had different gifts. We had different husbands who also had different gifts. In other words, we were designed to parent differently. It was easy to look at the other moms and think, *Why can't I be as content to be with my son as she is? Why does she seem happier than me?*

I was aware the transition back to the States would take a toll on our family but what I didn't consider was how much more it would impact me than my husband. Comparison convinced me that Erik was sailing through the move like water off a duck's back, while I wrestled emotionally and fell apart easily. It told me there must be something wrong with me if I could not pull myself together and enjoy life like he was.

Comparison kept my eyes fixed on my supposed shortcomings and prevented me from looking objectively at how different our realities were: most of Erik's job and relationships remained the same. We bought a house near the office, where he spent most of his time. While he enjoyed relative stability, I felt incompetent in navigating our new city. I reeled from the loss of relationships, and carried the bulk of the burden of helping our kids adjust to all changes.

No transition is the same. It does not matter if you and your sister-in-law have babies within days of each other; your transition to motherhood will be different. Maybe you moved to town at the same time as your neighbors, but that doesn't mean your journey is the same. We will only be discouraged if we compare. Sometimes the best encouragement we can give ourselves is to look at our situations with a strong dose of reality.

Social media makes it even harder for us to stay grounded in reality. It has given us a myriad of new ways to practice comparison. We compare our status updates, how our marriages are doing, how successful our children are, who got a new promotion, who's been on vacation (while we haven't). We monitor each other's home renovations, political views, and lifestyles. Here, we see the best of others' lives, and we tend to compare them to our worst, or at least our ordinary.

I remember seeing a new acquaintance on Facebook post pictures of herself at a birthday party with some women I knew enough to know I would enjoy a night out with them. Comparison grabbed my heart with the thought, *Why don't I get to go to fabulous parties like that yet?* Then I remembered: she's been here six years and I have been here six months.

Comparison that leads us to turn a negative eye on ourselves is the thief of joy, the destroyer of relationships, and an instrument of Satan to cause discontent in our hearts. It causes us to focus on our weaknesses, our losses, our lack. It often skews our ability to look at things objectively, to see that we are in our own unique situation that simply can't be measured next to someone else's. And it shuts us off from vulnerability because after all, how could someone who seems to be doing better than us ever understand how we're feeling?

God has a purpose for you in the situation you're in. When we look at someone else and wish for their situation, we can fall into rejecting the opportunities and gifts God has given us. We are saying it's not enough, it's not the best.

God has a different assignment for each of us, an assignment unique to each of us. He has different lessons to teach us, different things He wants to do in our hearts. He has something else for that other person. We can't let unhealthy comparison steal our focus, our joy, or our faith that this is for our good.

If we can find our grace givers, and move toward them with vulnerability, ignoring the lies of comparison that threaten to pull us apart, then there is a great opportunity presented to us. God wants to make us good traveling companions. He wants us to be wholehearted so that we too can lead others to whole-hearted living.

BECOMING THE GRACE GIVERS

One Sunday in church, our pastor asked us to raise our hands if we were currently experiencing a hard season. As hands around me rose, tears formed in my eyes. Compassion stirred in me. I wanted to gather every person together and say, "Okay listen, we can do this. I know it's hard, but we're in it together. God's got something good in store."

One of the greatest blessings of journeying through tough transitions is that they have the power to grow empathy in us. As we give ourselves permission to name where transition is hard for us, we give others permission to name their challenges. When we acknowledge our losses, we make space for others to acknowledge theirs. Naming our desires and honoring them as valid teaches us to honor others' desires. The more we do this, the more we will be the kind of people others need—not only in transition but in any trial of life. The more we make peace with change and learn to make God our anchor, the more we become the kind of people who can help others navigate what God is bringing them through. We will be people of grace and compassion, people who invite others on a path of freedom and restoration.

We are called to walk this road together. Transition can be a messy process, but a transformational one. If we want to navigate it quickly, then we can do it on our own, but we are bound to miss something in the process. If, instead, we want to see God redeem every aspect of what He is bringing us through, we must be anchored together.

THE GOSPEL IN TRANSITION

I was telling a friend of mine about this book and she asked me what it was I wanted to say. I told her, "When we own those places where we're struggling and recognize what's being stirred in us, a door opens to God meeting us in a deeper place. It's in transition that we learn to anchor ourselves more fully in who He is and His plans for us. I want people to see the reality of transition and how it impacts us. And then I want them to have hope."

She replied, "So what you're saying is: *You want the gospel.* You want death and you want life. If you try to live in one or the other, you miss part of the gospel. It's about asking: How do you willingly give yourself over to death, and how do you receive life? And what does it look like in transition?"

> Transition is an invitation to experience the gospel.

Transition is an invitation to experience the gospel. The gospel shows us that we cannot captain our own ships. We were never meant to. It tells us that there is despair, but there is hope. Something must die to make way for new life. The good news is that God uses transition to move us away from ourselves, away from our idols and false substitutes for life, and toward a greater dependence and rootedness in Him. Transition is a powerful tool in God's hands to show us where we need to let some things die, let others go, to own and embrace at a deep level God's truth and consistency in our lives.

I used to approach my heart like it was a vaguely familiar stranger, one whose name I wasn't sure of so I kept walking. I liked feeling put together and on top of life, and all that rose to the surface of my heart in transition slowed me down, and kept me from getting back to normal. And so I ignored it. Until I couldn't anymore.

I began to see how necessary it was. I began to pay attention to my heart, and honor it. And though good, it was only half the picture. We cannot simply look at our hearts without looking at them through the lens of God. We have to see them in light of who He is and what He can do in our lives. Otherwise, we miss the gospel in transition.

On many levels, transition can feel like death. We die to the idea that life is about being happy and comfortable, and instead look for God to show us His goodness. We let our false identities die and find a new way to live in the identity God has given us. We die to our own ways of satisfying desire and find new life in His strength. We die to the shape we believe our lives must take and watch Him bring purpose and meaning to us in unexpected ways.

In transition, when everything goes sideways, we have an opportunity for new life. There is no resurrection without death. But when we are willing to open our hands and offer the whole messy process to God, the Redeemer redeems.

In chapter 3, I talked about the two battles that wage in us, according to Frederick Buechner. This is the good news with which he closes his chapter:

Even if we do not find our place in the sun, or not quite the place we want, or a place where the sun is not as bright as we always dreamed that it would be, this is not the end because this is not really the decisive war, even though we spend so much of our lives assuming that it is.

The decisive war is the other one—to become fully human, which means to become compassionate, honest, brave. And this is a war against the darkness which no man fights alone. It is the war which every man can win who wills to win because it is the war which God also wills us to win and will arm us to win if only we will accept his armor. [3]

Making peace with change and clinging desperately to God is a battle. The enemy would love for transition and the emotions that are raised in it to shut us down. He would love us to harden our hearts, to become fearful and distrustful of God, to shore up our defenses so the next time around we won't hurt so much or we won't feel so much or we won't feel so lost.

We don't want him to win. Instead, we rest in the truth that God is greater than everything around us and in us. We let these emotions turn us toward Him with a hopeful gaze, with a childlike gaze that trusts that the Father knows what's going on, and has something unique for us to see.

In transition, we are given opportunity to embrace the gospel and the power of redemption. We bring every challenging, broken, and messy part of our hearts and lay them at His feet, where we trust Him to bring us to new life.

Acknowledgments

YEARS AGO, A FRIEND WHO READ MY BLOG TOLD me, "If you ever write a book, I would read it." Encouraging, but what should I write? It was our transition back to the U.S. that broke me apart and led me to begin writing more about the heart. It also caused me to reflect on how much God has done in me through every transition of my life. And as they say—write what you know.

The process was longer and harder than I anticipated, so I am deeply grateful for the voices who cheered me on as I went.

First, I am thankful to my husband, Erik. He has been my constant support and strength, has always made gracious space for me to pursue writing, and never hesitated when I suggested something that might help me in this pursuit.

I'm grateful to my whole family—my parents, siblings, and kids who have cheered me along the way. I couldn't find a bigger cheerleader than my mom, who never stopped believing this should be published or trying to find ways to help make it happen.

I'm indebted to my tribe of encouraging women—the ones who responded with love, encouragement, and prayer to my "I'm going to try to write today" texts—Jenny Higgins, Katie Watts, Kourtney Street, Alex Stecker, Iris Lowder, and Julie Ellis. I owe the inclusion of the chapter on expectations to Kourtney who, while we shopped in a Dillard's department store, insisted that I talk about it.

Thanks goes to Dayle Rogers for early reads and her unfailing encouragement that makes me believe I can do anything. Without the initial nudge and ongoing encouragement from Ken Cochrum to use my gift of writing, I don't know that I would have come this far. Thanks also to Judy Douglass for her writing wisdom and guidance, and for introducing me to the Redbud Writer's Guild.

Without that guild, this book would surely not exist. Thanks to all my Redbud sisters for their prayers, advice, editing help, launch team participation, and encouragement.

I'm indebted to Dawn Anderson and the team at Our Daily Bread Publishing for taking a chance on an unknown writer and for all their work to make this book happen.

Finally, I am grateful to Jesus for this opportunity and for the lessons He led me through to share in this book. Being able to see those lessons go out into the world through the words He's given me is such a humbling, undeserved gift.

Notes

CHAPTER 1. NAVIGATING THE HARD

1. Bruce Edstrom, "The Sleeping Heart," lecture, Hua Hin, Thailand, January 2012.
2. Dan B. Allender and Tremper Longman III, *The Cry of the Soul: How Our Emotions Reveal Our Deepest Questions About God* (Colorado Springs: NavPress, 1994), 139.
3. Bill Muehlenberg, "The Lament Psalms," *CultureWatch* (blog), February 2, 2012, http://billmuehlenberg.com/2012/02/02/the-lament-psalms/. Muehlenberg quotes Walter Brueggemann, *The Message of the Psalms: A Theological Commentary* (Minneapolis: Fortress Press, 1984), 78; and E. Calvin Beisner, *Psalms of Promise: Exploring the Majesty and Faithfulness of God* (Colorado Springs: NavPress, 1988), 57.
4. D. A. Carson, *How Long, O Lord?: Reflections on Suffering and Evil*, 2nd ed. (Grand Rapids: Baker Academic, 2006), 67.

Chapter 2. Anchored in His Goodness

1. Brent Curtis and John Eldredge, *The Sacred Romance: Drawing Closer to the Heart of God* (Nashville, TN: Thomas Nelson, Inc., 1997), 33.

Chapter 3. Navigating Loss

1. More than six years later, I still have a regular prayer time with friends overseas through Google chat. It's challenging to coordinate between several time zones, but I don't want to let go of this connection!
2. Timothy Keller with Kathy Keller, *The Meaning of Marriage: Facing the Complexities of Commitment with the Wisdom of God* (New York: Penguin Books, 2011), 101.
3. Frederick Buechner, *The Magnificent Defeat* (New York: Harper & Row, 1985), 37.
4. Janice Y.K. Lee, *The Expatriates* (New York: Penguin Books, 2016), 105. I don't recommend this book for everyone. It was relevant to me in that season of my life because we had been transplanted to Asia.

Chapter 4. Anchored in What Is Constant

1. Stacey Thacker and Brooke McGlothlin, *Hope for the Weary Mom: Let God Meet You in the Mess* (Eugene, OR: Harvest House, 2015), 51.
2. Brennan Manning, *Abba's Child: The Cry of the Heart for Intimate Belonging* (Colorado Springs: NavPress, 2002), 64.
3. Sarah Bessey, *Jesus Feminist: An Invitation to Revisit the Bible's View of Women* (New York: Howard Books, 2013), 114.
4. C. S. Lewis, *The Problem of Pain* (San Francisco: HarperOne, 2009), 117.

Chapter 5. Navigating Desire

1. Anne Lamott, *Bird by Bird: Some Instructions on Writing and Life* (New York: Anchor Books, 1995), 180.
2. Brené Brown, *I Thought It Was Just Me (But It Isn't): Making the Journey From "What Will People Think?" to "I Am Enough"* (New York: Gotham Books, 2007), 55.
3. Dan Allender, *The Wounded Heart: Hope for Adult Victims of Childhood Sexual Abuse* (Colorado Springs: NavPress, 2018), 79–80.
4. Paula Reinhart, *Strong Women, Soft Hearts: A Woman's Guide to Cultivating a Wise Heart and a Passionate Life* (Nashville: Thomas Nelson, 2001), 105.
5. *Thanks for Sharing*, directed by Stuart Blumberg (Santa Monica, CA: Lionsgate, 2012).

Chapter 6. Anchored in His Strength

1. C. S. Lewis, *A Grief Observed* (San Francisco: HarperOne, 2009), 40.
2. Paula Reinhart, *Strong Women, Soft Hearts: A Woman's Guide to Cultivating a Wise Heart and a Passionate Life* (Nashville: Thomas Nelson, 2001), 105.
3. John Ortberg, *Soul Keeping: Caring for the Most Important Part of You* (Grand Rapids, MI: Zondervan, 2014), 82.
4. C. S. Lewis, *Letters of C. S. Lewis* (Eugene, OR: Harvest Books, 2003), 220.

Chapter 7. Navigating Expectations

1. M. Craig Barnes, *When God Interrupts: Finding New Life through Unwanted Change* (Madison, WI: InterVarsity Press, 1996), 116.

Chapter 8. Staying Anchored

1. Paula Reinhart, *Strong Women, Soft Hearts: A Woman's Guide to Cultivating a Wise Heart and a Passionate Life* (Nashville: Thomas Nelson, 2001), 77, 79.

2. Tammy Maltby, *The God Who Sees You: Look to Him When You Feel Discouraged, Forgotten, or Invisible* (Colorado Springs: David C. Cook, 2012), 119.

3. Stacey Thacker and Brooke McGlothlin, *Hope for the Weary Mom: Let God Meet You in the Mess* (Eugene, OR: Harvest House, 2015), 141.

4. Kristen Strong, *Girl Meets Change: Truths to Carry You through Life's Transitions* (Ada, MI: Baker, 2015), 110.

5. Jan Meyers, *The Allure of Hope: God's Pursuit of a Woman's Heart* (Colorado Springs: NavPress, 2001), 146–47.

6. Paul Miller, *A Praying Life: Connecting with God in a Distracting World* (Colorado Springs: NavPress, 2009), 185–86.

7. Tammy Maltby, *The God Who Sees You: Look to Him When You Feel Discouraged, Forgotten, or Invisible* (Colorado Springs: David C. Cook, 2012), 121.

Chapter 9. Navigating Grief

1. *Inside Out*, directed by Pete Docter (Emeryville, CA: Pixar, 2015).

2. J.R. Forasteros, "Inside Out: The Gift of Grief," NorvilleRogers .com-News from Coolsville (blog), June 22, 2015, https://www .norvillerogers.com/inside-out-the-gift-of-grief/.

3. Michael Card, *A Sacred Sorrow: Reaching Out to God in the Lost Language of Lament* (Colorado Springs: NavPress, 2005), 137.

4. *Shadowlands*, directed by Richard Attenborough (Price Entertainment, 1993).

5.   J.R. Forasteros, "Inside Out: The Gift of Grief," NorvilleRogers
     .com-News from Coolsville (blog), June 22, 2015. https://www
     .norvillerogers.com/inside-out-the-gift-of-grief/

6.   "Grieving Well: I Can Hold Loss," UMission (blog), accessed March
     19, 2019, http://umission.org/lessons/grieving-well-i-can-hold-loss/.

CHAPTER 10. ANCHORED TOGETHER

1.   Brené Brown, "The Power of Vulnerability," CHP Leaders Blog
     (blog), June 6, 2017, https://sites.uci.edu/chpleaders/2017/06/06
     /brene-brown-the-power-of-vulnerability/.

2.   Jeff Brown, *Ascending with Both Feet on the Ground: Words to Awaken
     Your Heart* (Acton, Ontario: Enrealment Press, 2012), 115.

3.   Frederick Buechner, *The Magnificent Defeat* (New York: Harper &
     Row, 1985), 43.

Help us get the word out!

Our Daily Bread Publishing exists to feed the soul with the Word of God.

If you appreciated this book, please let others know.

- Pick up another copy to give as a gift.
- Share a link to the book or mention it on social media.
- Write a review on your blog, on a book-seller's website, or at our own site (ourdailybreadpublishing.org).
- Recommend this book for your church, book club, or small group.

Connect with us:

 @ourdailybread

 @ourdailybread

 @ourdailybread

Our Daily Bread Publishing
PO Box 3566
Grand Rapids, Michigan 49501 USA

✉ books@odb.org